Countering Suicide Terrorism
An International Conference

February 20-23, 2000

Herzliya, Israel

The International Policy Institute for
Counter-Terrorism

at the

Interdisciplinary Center Herzliya

International Policy Institute for Counter-Terrorism
P.O. Box 167
Herzliya 46150, Israel

ISBN 965-90365-1-5

 **www.israelbooks.com**

JERUSALEM ◆ NEW YORK

MAIN OFFICE IN ISRAEL:
GEFEN PUBLISHING HOUSE LTD.
P.O.B. 36004, JERUSALEM 91360
TEL: 972-2-538-0247
Fax: 972-2-538-8423
E-Mail: info@gefenpublishing.com

U.S.A. OFFICE:
GEFEN BOOKS
12 NEW ST, HEWLETT, NY 11557
TEL: 1-516-295-2805
FAX: 1-516-295-2739
E-Mail: gefenbooks@compuserve.com

Countering Suicide Terrorism:
An International Conference

PSYCHOLOGICAL AND SOCIOLOGICAL DIMENSIONS OF SUICIDE TERRORISM

Preface

Over the past two decades a number of nations have been forced to contend with the phenomenon of suicide terrorism. Such diverse countries as Turkey, Sri Lanka, Israel and the United States have all been targets for effective suicide attacks against densely populated civilian and military targets.

Suicide terrorism constitutes a significant escalation in terrorist activity. In his ability to implement the attack at precisely the time and place where it will cause the maximum number of casualties and greatest damage, the suicide bomber is virtually guaranteed success. Even the least deadly of such attacks succeed in striking a devastating blow to public morale.

Suicide terrorism is all the more threatening because of the difficulties of combating it, the large number of casualties it creates, and the religious and ideological zeal it inspires. It is a phenomenon that often, though not always, goes hand in hand with religious extremism—distorting religion in the service of political aims.

ICT's Second International Conference: Countering Suicide Terrorism

In order to find ways of combating the phenomenon of suicide terrorism, the International Policy Institute for Counter-Terrorism (ICT) held an international conference on the subject in February 2000 at the Interdisciplinary Center (IDC), in Herzliya, Israel.

The Conference, *Countering Suicide Terrorism,* brought together academic experts and counter-terrorism professionals from all over the world in a multi-disciplinary venue to compare ways and means of countering the threat of suicide terrorism. Lecturers included experts from Israel, the Palestinian Authority, Turkey, Sri Lanka, the United Kingdom and the United States.

The Opening Ceremony of the Conference was held at the Interdisciplinary Center and was attended by dignitaries from Israel and abroad. Speakers included Shabtai Shavit, Chairman of ICT's Board of Directors; Prof. Uriel Reichman, President of IDC; Yael German, Mayor of Herzliya; Yosef Maiman, Chairman of ICT's

Board of Trustees; Admiral (ret.) Fulvio Martini, Former Head of the Italian Intelligence Service; and General (ret.) Amnon Lipkin-Shahak, Israeli Minister of Tourism and Former Chief of Staff of the Israel Defense Forces.

The Open Conference

The first day of the Conference was devoted to examining the roots of suicide terrorism as a historical phenomenon, and was divided into two sessions. The morning session dealt with International Terrorism and was chaired by Prof. Ehud Sprinzak, Dean of the Lauder School of Government at IDC. Speakers included Prof. Uzi Arad; terrorism expert Prof. Martha Crenshaw; Dr. Ely Karmon, Director of ICT's database project; and Frank Anderson, former Head of the CIA's Near East Division. This session examined the growth of suicide terrorism and showed how the phenomenon fit in with other operational methods of terrorism.

The afternoon session dealt with Fundamentalist Terrorism and was chaired by Ambassador Michael Sheehan, Coordinator for Counter-Terrorism at the U.S. Department of State. The session examined the phenomenon of radical religious terrorism, focusing primarily on Islamist suicide terrorism. Lectures were given by Professor Abdul Hadi Palazzi, Director of the Cultural Institute of the Italian Islamic Community in Rome; Yoram Schweitzer, director of ICT's educational project; and ICT's academic director, Reuven Paz.

The second day of the Conference dealt with the particulars of suicide terrorism, from both the geographical and sociological perspectives. The first session was chaired by Professor Martha Crenshaw of Wesleyan University, U.S.A. The session focused on the Characteristics of Suicide Terrorism Worldwide and included case studies of suicide terrorism in Sri Lanka, Turkey, Lebanon and Israel. Lecturers included Dr. Rohan Gunaratna of the Center for the Study of Terrorism and Political Violence at the University of St. Andrews, Scotland; Professor Dogu Ergil, of Ankara University in Turkey; ICT Research Fellow Dr. Shaul Shay; and Boaz Ganor, Executive Director of ICT.

The afternoon session dealt with the Psychological and Sociological Dimensions of Suicide Terrorism. This session was chaired by Professor Barry Rubin, the Deputy Director of the BESA Center for Strategic Studies at Bar Ilan University. Lectures were given by Professor Israel Orbach of Bar Ilan University, who discussed suicide from a psychological perspective; and by Dr. Khalil Shiqaqi, Head of the Center for Palestine Research and Studies in Nablus, who discussed the views of Palestinian society on suicide terrorism.

The Closed Seminar

The last day of the Conference consisted of a closed seminar for security professionals from Israel and abroad to compare notes and discuss possible solutions. This session was closed to the media and the general public, in order to allow participants to address more sensitive concerns. The closed session concluded with the formulation of a policy paper summing up some of the principal issues that must be addressed in order to combat suicide terrorism. The text of this policy paper may be found as Appendix I.

Acknowledgments

We would like to thank all those who helped to make the Conference a success, beginning with ICT's administrative staff: Ayelet Soltz-Landau, Pnina Yarden, Irit Mor, Gal Perlov, and Alex Grey. The staff of the Interdisciplinary Center, Herzliya, contributed greatly to the success of the Conference—especially Tami Zadok, who lent us her considerable public-relations skills. The following companies and organizations donated funds or services to the Conference: The Rich Foundation for Education & Welfare, El Al Israel Airlines, Klal Insurance, Israeli Phoenix, Netvision, and the Public Affairs Office of the Embassy of the United States of America in Israel. Lastly, we would like to thank Yael Shahar for editing the text of the lectures and preparing the manuscript for publication.

Boaz Ganor
Executive Director
International Policy Institute for Counter-Terrorism

5

Introduction

Amnon Lipkin-Shahak

General (ret.), Minister of Tourism, Former Chief of Staff, Israel Defense Forces

I believe that there are several people in this room who have had personal experience with terrorism. I do not remember the exact date of my first encounter with terrorists. I think it was in the mid-50's, when I was a young Lieutenant. As I recall, at that time we attacked the first terrorist bases in cities that are now very familiar to Israel—Jenin, Kalkilya, and later on Samora. These cities not only served as bases for terrorist attacks but also provided a haven for terrorists.

We all recall the attacks that have taken place over the last few years; those perpetrated through suicide terror. I believe that these attacks were motivated by desperation.

However, I would like to address another question today, namely: Can peace agreements bring an end to terror activities in the Middle East?

Historically, the first person to commit suicide while taking the lives of many others was Samson. He was not a terrorist, nor was his act a terror attack. He was being held prisoner by the Philistines then; he had been tortured, his eyes had been gouged out, and he knew he was soon to die anyway. And although he was unable to see anything, he nonetheless gathered some information. Through listening to the voices around him he realized that he was being held in a palace full of his enemies. He asked someone to guide him to the exact spot that would enable him, in a single act and with the help of God, to bring his life to an end as well as the lives of his enemies. And he performed this act out of rage, because he thirsted for revenge, and because he was desperate.

By its very nature, I believe that suicide terrorism, as it is perpetrated by certain terrorists, is motivated by desperation. Perhaps they seek revenge, or maybe someone promised them a place in Heaven. There can be no doubt that many of them are incited by religious preachers. But the basic reason for this act is desperation, and the feeling that they have reached a dead end.

Samson had no other choice. However, the terrorists have other choices. Even those who choose to commit suicide terror independently, and certainly those who are commanded to do so.

We in the IDF, witnessed the first suicide terror attacks in Lebanon in '83. This came as a result of the Lebanon War, which was followed by the establishment of the previously unknown Hizballah. We originally set out to fight the PLO in Lebanon, but ended up battling the Hizballah. From the very beginning, the Hizballah initiated terror attacks or suicide terror attacks on Israeli and non-Israeli targets. As we all recall, and as stated before, attacks of this kind were launched against American troops in Beirut and other targets there. Their objective was to arouse world interest, cause a large number of casualties among all those in the vicinity, and score points in the international arena. Ten years later we began to witness other terror attacks, or suicide terror attacks, initiated by Palestinians against Israeli targets. I believe this trend started in '93. To begin with, these attacks were not very sophisticated. Only after the massacre perpetrated by Baruch Goldstein in Hebron, did some of these suicide missions become more sophisticated.

I would describe the course of events as follows: It took twenty five years of continuous terror attacks committed by Palestinians against Israel and Israeli targets, both inside and outside of Israel (which were handled with a significant degree of success by the various Israeli security organizations), before they started to initiate suicide terror attacks inside Israel and the Territories.

Why did the process take so long? I have no idea. Did the Hizballah serve as an example or provide motivation? Perhaps.

Who were these Palestinians? They consisted mainly of two organizations—the Hamas and the Islamic Jihad. Regardless of these murderous attacks, I think that if we study the history of terror against Israel, it becomes evident that the issue of Israeli prisoners being held hostage by terrorist organizations has a greater impact on Israeli public opinion, on the Israeli government, and on the Israeli decision-making process than any other. I believe that this kind of activity is much more influential in the long run. The present policy of some of the organizations (particularly but not only in Lebanon) to take Israeli hostages derives from the lessons they have learned from the history of terror attacks against Israel. We all remember when Ahmed Jibril exchanged a handful of Israeli soldiers for thousands of terrorists, of whom more than a few went back to active terrorism almost immediately after their release. The Israeli willingness to pay such a steep price in order to release the hostages or the prisoners undoubtedly impaired our deterrence level and our perceived commitment to fight terrorism. For various reasons, the terror organizations were subsequently forced to change their methods—not because they did not want to capture Israeli prisoners, but because in most cases they were unsuccessful in achieving this goal.

Without a doubt, it is clear that the suicidal attacks, especially those committed in late '95 and early '96, had a dramatic impact on the Israelis and on their willingness to continue the peace process with the Palestinians. And there is no doubt that the suicidal attack reflects determination, cruelty, deep conviction, and desperation.

The question, then, is if the peace process and signed peace agreements can effectively diminish the feeling of desperation among our enemies. I pose this question and I shall endeavor to provide an answer. More specifically, can a peace agreement now between Syria and Israel, and between the Palestinians and Israel, bring an end to the terror and suicidal terrorism against Israel? This is another question that I will endeavor to answer.

There remain two fronts on which we fight terrorist activities, terror, and guerrilla warfare. The first is the Palestinian front. In this case, the terrorists plan and execute their missions from inside the areas under the control of the Palestinian Authority. The terror is perpetrated only by Palestinians, mainly from the Hamas and the Islamic Jihad organizations. Its main mission is to forestall a peace agreement between Israel and the Palestinian Authority. They (particularly the Hamas) and their operators regard an agreement of this sort as a form of surrender to the Israelis, to the Israeli government, without any regard for their legitimate rights. In Lebanon it is more a case of guerilla warfare initiated by Shihads (martyrs) associated with the Hizballah. The latter organization enjoys the support of the Iranians and the Syrians, who declare that the aim of their activities is to bring an end to the Israéli occupation of South Lebanon. However, their declarations reflect a kind of ambiguity vis-a-vis their intentions if and when Israel withdraws its forces to the international border. This is not an oversight. Among the Palestinians, I have no doubt that there will remain a number of elements that will be completely dissatisfied after any peace agreement that we might sign. There is no doubt that the Palestinians will have to agree to concessions on almost every issue—on the question of Jerusalem, on the borders, on Israeli settlements, as well as on the matter of the refugees. And therefore, I believe that those extreme elements will feel dissatisfied with any agreement, and will continue to try and launch their attacks against Israel and Israeli targets in order to achieve their goal.

Here the question arises: To what extent will the Palestinian population cooperate with the Palestinian Authority in condemning these acts? This is a major issue that will need to be faced by Israel and the Palestinians. The greater the progress in the peace negotiations, the more cooperation we stand to gain among Palestinians against terror attacks perpetrated by fellow Palestinians. In the event of failure or serious obstacles in the Israeli-Palestinian dialogue, we might face a totally different situation. In that case we will not be dealing only with the Hamas or the Islamic Jihad. We might even witness entities who are now a part of or connected to the Palestinian Authority, turning their backs on the process and reverting to terror activities against Israel. And if this is indeed the scenario, we can assume that the kind of activities that you are going to discuss over the next two days may become even more common and more popular among the Palestinian people.

Even in Lebanon we must face a serious question: Can withdrawal to the international border bring an end to the Hizballah activities? No one in Israel would argue that if this is a surefire solution, then unilateral withdrawal is a must and cannot be delayed. But the question continues to loom because of declarations by Hizballah leaders, who state that they will continue to fight against Israel until Jerusalem is liberated. Additionally, there is the issue of Hizballah's ability to withstand Iranian and Syrian pressure that could well increase if the peace talks between Israel and Syria fail. The Hizballah's heavy dependence on Iran's political, military and economic support plays a central role here.

On the other hand, I believe that if we do achieve a peace agreement with Syria, the latter will be forced to commit to disarming the Hizballah. I doubt if this will be easy. I doubt if the Hizballah is going to cooperate with the Syrians in achieving this end. But in this case, I think that Syria will have no other choice but to go ahead and disarm the Hizballah.

I would like to remind you all that in the late '80's, when there was some tension between the Hizballah and Syria about activities in Lebanon, the Hizballah attacked Syrian targets on the Syrian-Lebanese border, and they could do so again. However I believe not only that Israel will demand Hizballah's disarmament, but that this must be a part of any Israeli-Syrian peace agreement. Once the Hizballah is disarmed, the legitimate forces of the Lebanese government can be stationed along the international border and security border.

Thus, I fear that suicide terrorism is the kind of act that we may be forced to face in the future too. Therefore, we must be ready to contend with it, while bearing in mind that this is not the only nor the most deadly or the most painful terrorist activity that we may be forced to face in the future. And the better we are prepared, the fewer casualties we will sustain and the fewer terror attacks we will have to contend with, in Israel and abroad, against Israeli and Jewish targets.

International Terrorism

Session Chairman: Prof. Ehud Sprinzak, Dean of
Lauder School of Government, IDC; ICT Board
of Directors, Israel

Do Nations Commit Suicide?
A Middle Eastern Perspective

Uzi Arad

Director, Institute of Policy and Strategy, The Interdisciplinary Center, Herzliya

The focus of this conference is on suicide terrorism. The level of analysis—to employ a political-science term—is the individual terrorist or the terrorist organization, and governments, only in so far as it pertains to cooperation in combating terrorism. I want to focus on a different level of analysis: that of the state, and various kinds of suicidal conduct and terror at the state level.

The question I chose to put to myself is the following: Is there a discontinuity between the prevalence of suicidal behavior and the effects of terror on the sub-state and state levels? Because the argument is often heard that while individuals may practice suicide terrorism, states do not. That is, if true, a very reassuring proposition, particularly in light of the common concern about the possible linking of terrorists and weapons of mass destruction. Terrorists may have difficulty obtaining weapons of mass destruction; states much less so.

But is the argument about states not practicing suicide terror valid? Of the two attributes, suicide and terror, it is the suicidal streak that requires greater attention, for few would question whether states commit acts of terror; because when broadly defined and not in the sense of supporting terrorist organizations, they all have done or currently do so. It is the suicidal trait, then, that will be the focus of my observations.

Technically speaking, states commit suicide in the sense that leaders are perfectly capable of sending their subjects to their deaths on so-called suicidal missions. The phenomenon is mostly confined to non-democracies, for example, the Japanese kamikaze, to which I shall return. But there have also been one-way bombing missions sanctioned by democracies. The examples of such missions, which are purely suicidal, are numerous, and so are the examples of cases in which the acceptance of purely suicidal missions is extolled by democracies. A good war recruit often involves this kind of acceptance. Not surprisingly, the reasons for the use of this kind of suicidal mission by states do not differ from the reasons terrorist organizations use it: considerations of efficiency, ease of delivery, precision in targeting, and so forth.

There is another special case in which suicide of a totally different type is employed by states, and that is the act of self-destruction by a leader, usually in the face of ultimate defeat and possible death. Let's call this "preemptive suicide." Amnon Lipkin-Shachak has alluded to the "Samson model." But while such a model has a retaliatory element, let us reflect for a minute on another biblical model, "the Saul model," which is preemptive rather than retaliatory.

Consider for a moment the Hitler precedent. That case is suggestive first because, interestingly enough, the OSS psychologist Langer predicted it years before it happened. And secondly, because it was not only Hitler who committed suicide, but also Eva Braun and the Goebbels family. The Samson model is concerned with suicide and its relation to affairs of state. Now that is a much more complicated model and refers to an act of suicide, which is at once both preemptive *and* retaliatory. Moreover, the retaliatory part entails the inflicting of greater punishment on others than that sustained by the person committing suicide. And it is at this juncture, perhaps, that the intriguing query presents itself: When does a leader facing his inevitable demise opt for a Saul model of departure, and when does he opt for the Samson model? That could be a critical question for future contingencies. It could come to haunt intelligence analysts when they ponder conditions in which leaders face their demise.

But let us for a moment also consider the historical question: Why, indeed, didn't Hitler depart with a big bang, given the fact that he possessed the capacity to inflict great damage, having chemical and possibly biological arsenals? The answer to that interesting question, as far as I can tell, is that Hitler never adopted a policy threatening the use of such capabilities, neither in war nor for the purposes of deterrence. Therefore, the option did not actually present itself operationally—and possibly not even logistically—when the need arose.

"The March of Folly"

I come now to a totally different category of what could be construed as essentially suicidal behavior: what I call "the March of Folly Syndrome." This takes place in cases where nations, half-knowingly—with what psychologists might describe as "sub-intentionally suicidal behavior"—tumble into catastrophe. This takes us back to the First World War, which, interestingly enough, has been described by many historians in suicidal terms. For example, Alan Clark entitled his book *Battles on the Eastern Front: Suicide of Empires.* What he meant was the way three empires—Germany, Austria-Hungary and Russia—exhausted themselves to the point of collapse on the eastern front. Barbara Tuchman, who coined the phrase "the March of Folly," is another historian of that war, and she describes best in that book the almost tragically inevitable drift into what could ultimately be suicide for some empires and states.

Coming back to the Second World War and the deliberate use of suicide attacks, I want to take a fresh, hard look at the kamikaze syndrome, before turning to two other examples. The story is familiar. Japan has a tradition of glorifying suicide; the training of kamikaze began at the outset of the war, and they were used extensively in the last stages as well. What is often overlooked is the secondary suicidal development that occurred. It may well have been unintended, but it was suicidal nonetheless: Not only did the kamikaze accomplish their mission by causing significant damage and terrorizing U.S. carriers and American forces; they also convinced American leaders that Japan would fight to the last soldier if and when the United States invaded Japan proper.

That realization, in turn, persuaded American leaders—who had developed atomic weapons for use against Germany, not Japan— that they would have to use the bomb against Japan. And for Japan, what began as a deliberate and possibly desperate use of a limited

16

course of suicide attacks, ended with an unintended consequence of devastating proportions.

Suicidal behavior in the Cold War

Interestingly enough, however, what occurred during the Second World War as a sub-intended or quasi-suicidal condition had by the time of the Cold War, with nuclear weapons on both sides, crystallized into institutional suicidal behavior and led to the adoption of suicidal doctrines by both sides. Because, as we all know—and there is no point in dwelling on this at length here—it is the predicament of nuclear deterrent strategies that they depend on the mutual threat of suicide. In its purest form this is known as "mutual assured destruction," and in its popular form as "the balance of *terror.*"

That posture, whether based on present technologies or those that prevailed at the end of the Second World War, is built around the threat of self-destruction. It is the logic of deterrence that the effective way to sustain survival depends on a credible threat to commit mass suicide under certain extreme contingencies—whether under the slogan, "better dead than red," or in the context of the Samson model of punishment as applied to deterrence. The inherent paradox of deterrence is that what is rational *ex-anti* depends on the threat of an irrational act *ex-post.* And the corollary of the deterrence paradox, when taken to its ultimate conclusion, was the adoption of the anti-ballistic missile treaty that practically ensured that suicide would occur if and when deterrence failed. This is, in a way, another form of suicide terrorism. It is the balance of terror predicated on a willingness to commit suicide under certain conditions.

When analysts searched for theoretical models that would yield approximations of how conduct in a nuclear crisis might develop, they adopted the adolescent game of chicken, clearly one of attempted suicidal or quasi-suicidal behavior with the additional concept of recklessness. And, in fact, these models saw the balance of terror as the rational practice of recklessness to accomplish certain political purposes.

Let us take a fresh look at another example, which is perhaps the archetypal case of a nuclear crisis: the Cuban Missile Crisis. Even the initial post-crisis accounts described it as a "damn near thing," with either McGeorge Bundy or Robert McNamara saying that at the time they reckoned that the probability of an escalation to nuclear exchange was something like twenty or thirty percent. But now, many years after the fact, we have far more information at our disposal, including the secret Kennedy tapes as well as the revised histories such as the Fusenco and Naftali book, *One Hell of a Gamble* (as indeed it was), together with the Alison Anzalico revision of *Essence of Decision*. It is now clear that the Russian roulette played over Cuba had far more bullets in the chamber than even Bundy or McNamara estimated at the time. Contrary to the initial glorifying descriptions by Arthur Schlesinger and others of the crisis management as "brilliantly controlled and matchlessly calibrated," McNamara now concedes that the decision-making process in Washington, as well as in Moscow and Havana, was characterized by "misinformation, miscalculation and misjudgment." Theodore Sorenson, more recently, said that despite all the management efforts at the time, the crisis came close to spinning out of control before it was luckily ended.

Some examples to justify these claims: In the early nineties it emerged that the Soviets had deployed tactical nuclear missiles in Cuba to be used against the United States should it invade Cuba. Secondly, and much more ominously, Soviet field commanders in Cuba had pre-delegated authority to use those tactical missiles without further direction from the Kremlin.

Now, as for asking what might have happened had the United States invaded Cuba, as some advisers had consistently recommended to Kennedy throughout the crisis, just ask yourself. Surely, no one believes that U.S. troops could have been attacked by tactical nuclear warheads without the United States responding, probably massively, with nuclear warheads against Russia. And where would that have ended? In utter disaster.

Consider in retrospect the sequence of suicidal steps, each step of the way. First, the very introduction of IRBMs by the Russians into Cuba was a classic March of Folly action, as Sherman Kent, an American intelligence analyst, said at the time. And he was right conceptually. Second, Soviet pre-delegation of the authority to use tactical nuclear weapons to field commanders was highly reckless, highly destabilizing and practically suicidal. Third, the U.S. considered an invasion that certainly would have triggered a tactical Russian response. Fourth, in response to this kind of tactical use, the United States would probably have opted for strategic retaliation, with all the calamitous effects that would have followed.

Presumably, lessons ought to have been learned from that crisis, which appeared so close to nuclear exchange. And indeed, all kinds of lessons have been learned from the Cuban missile crisis, ranging from the introduction of a hot-line to efforts to introduce greater flexibility into the doctrine of deterrence by McNamara and others. Still, as we have learned only recently, some of the most destabilizing aspects of that situation continued. For example, we now know that the practice of pre-delegation was continued and applied on the American side; NATO field commanders in the European Theater had similar authority well into the Eighties.

Decapitation and the Middle East

There was yet another doctrinal spin that took place in the late Seventies and early Eighties: the consideration of a strategy of "decapitation," that is, hitting the leaders of the other side and the entire regime. That in itself, if the other side possesses weapons of mass destruction, almost invites a Samson-like response; and, if coupled with a pre-delegated doctrine on the other side, almost guarantees it—which brings us closer to our times and to our region, to Saddam Hussein and Iraq.

Saddam Hussein, too, pre-delegated to his divisional commanders in 1990 the authority to use chemical weapons should communications with Baghdad be cut. Saddam blundered initially and prematurely into occupying Kuwait. He then miscalculated the American response; but from then on, what he did, including the adoption of a pre-delegated practice—perhaps deliberately so that the other side would know—was in fact a very consistent and very rational employment of deterrence. So it is not at him that one should look with some degree of concern. Reflect, rather, for a moment—what would have happened had the coalition marched on Baghdad, as some advisers proposed, very much as other advisers years before had proposed a march on Havana. Under conditions of pre-delegation that could have been folly indeed. How would Saddam have acted in the face of an advancing army? One can only guess. How would he have reacted had his survival been put at risk? One could also ask how his divisional commanders would have acted in his absence. Any contemplation of these contingencies that takes into account an adversary with his back to the wall and who possesses weapons of mass destruction, suggests that what we are dealing with is, in fact, an exercise in suicide or variations thereof.

More recently, the United States adopted a declared policy of trying to tackle the Saddam regime which even included the firing of Tomahawk cruise missiles against regime targets. Here in Israel, government spokesmen began referring explicitly to the possibility of an extreme contingency, in which Saddam, with his back to the wall, might fire his residual chemical or biological capabilities at Israel. Such analysis, near as I can tell, is certainly coherent, since with nothing to lose, all restraints on Saddam would fall away and the above scenario could very well develop. But if decapitating Saddam could lead to the same result, then a strategy aiming at such a result must be characterized as extremely risky. And to the extent that Saddam himself, either tacitly or explicitly, has been fanning such fears to prevent an attack on him, his strategy has actually been one of prudence. Indeed, Saddam's strategy under these conditions seems to be relatively sensible.

Conclusions

In taking a new look at some of these examples—Japan, the Cuban missile crisis, and Iraq—we come back to the question I posed at the outset: Is there a practice of quasi- or sub-intentional suicidal policies on the state level?

It seems that although the phenomenon occurs in different ways and forms, the interplay between human behavior, technological advances and the acquisition of weapons of mass destruction has made it a phenomenon that does exist at the level of states, just as it exists on the sub-state level. Suicidal and sub-intentional suicidal pathologies may be inherent in the actions of certain human beings, hence human folly when such people are at the helm of state. Suicidal strategies may also be intrinsic to the rationale of deterrence through a balance of terror, or in the management of a confrontation with a leader who possesses the capacity to inflict massive damage.

These are the disturbing thoughts with which I conclude my discourse over that original question: Is terrorism and suicide terrorism just a matter of the individual terrorist and organization, or is it applicable also to the realm of state behavior?

"Suicide" Terrorism in Comparative Perspective

Martha Crenshaw

Professor, Wesleyan University

Acts of terrorism that require the death of the perpetrator for successful implementation, typically known as "suicide" attacks, represent the intersection of separate historical trends in terrorism. Although the tactic may present itself as unique and innovative, it is a combination of familiar methods, targets, and motives. Thus suicide terrorism should be interpreted as a particular case of oppositional terrorism rather than as a *sui generis* phenomenon. It shares many of the properties of general terrorism.

For example, the characteristic phenomenon of the 1980's and 1990's in Sri Lanka, Turkey, Lebanon, and Israel is basically a form of bombing, which is the favored method of terrorism, accounting for about half of all incidents. Terrorist bombings originated in the late 19th century, facilitated by the invention of dynamite. The Russian revolutionaries used bombs as a tool for the assassination of public figures, including most prominently the Czar in 1881. Irish republicans used bombs to attack public transportation and symbolic targets in London, although casualties were rare. Anarchist bombings were directed at anonymous civilians in public places, such as restaurants. With technological advances and increased availability of explosives, bombings became commonplace in struggles such as the Algerian war for independence. The "Battle of Algiers," 1956-1957, featured bombs in cafes, bars, restaurants, and sports stadiums, as well as at bus stops and on beaches. Random civilian casualties among the European population were the hallmark of the FLN's terrorist campaign.

Why are bombings favored? Many answers would focus on considerations of material convenience. Even the most destructive bombs can be quite simple to manufacture. Simplicity is an attribute in many suicide bombings, since the terrorist agent acts as the detonator, thus obviating the need for a sophisticated timing device. Yet bombs must undoubtedly have an intrinsic emotional appeal as well.

In general, bombings are often unclaimed. In fact, from the terrorist point of view one of their advantages is that the perpetrators have a good chance of avoiding detection. Risk for the organization and the individual can be kept low. The perpetrators of suicide attacks, however, forfeit anonymity, although sponsoring organizations (such as the LTTE) may not claim credit.

Bombings, like all acts of terrorism, pose not only an immediate danger but also threaten future harm. Each bombing establishes the expectation that more will follow. However, bombings are distinguished from the second major form of terrorism, hostage-taking. Hostage-taking, which represented a genuine innovation in terrorism, is a more explicit form of compellence because it involves an ultimatum. A time deadline is imposed, setting limits within which compliance by the government must be produced. Such actions include kidnappings, aircraft hijackings, and barricade situations. By the 1990's this form of open bargaining with governments diminished, while bombings continue to be popular.

The global rise and decline of hostage-taking suggests the possibility of cyclical patterns of terrorism. Cycles of terrorism may well be related to processes of geographical contagion or diffusion, as new strategies of terrorism are disseminated across national borders. Terrorism, for example, spread from Latin America and the Middle East to Western Europe in the 1970's. The reasons for this transmission included a shared ideology of anti-Americanism and anti-imperialism among radical groups, deliberate imitation of "third world" revolutionary tactics by West European organizations, and spill-over effects due to physical contacts and relationships of mutual convenience, especially with Palestinian groups after the Munich Olympics attack of 1972. Thus the process of diffusion involved both learning, which could be long-distance, and active cooperation.

Within specific campaigns of terrorism, there are also identifiable patterns of development. For example, the scope of what constitutes an acceptable target for terrorism is often progressively widened. This broadening of the target group may be the result of the erosion of moral inhibitions. Sometimes it seems to be caused by leaders' loss of control over their followers. This trend, in which terrorism appears to evolve toward less discrimination in the selection of targets, might also be related to what is known as the displacement or substitution effect. Sandler and Lapan analyze the choice of targets in non-bargaining situations.[1] Assuming that terrorists are rational individuals, operating under resource constraints, they can attack only one country. If that potential target increases its defensive measures, terrorism will shift to a different target. On the basis of formal modeling, Sandler and Lapan predict a displacement effect. That is, effective unilateral counter-measures by one state will increase the vulnerability of other states who do not or cannot take such measures. Thus terrorists' choices are sensitive primarily to what governments do to protect themselves.

Similarly, Enders, Sandler, and Cauley describe a substitution effect: when new technologies or policies are applied to prevent specific kinds of terrorist events, terrorists transfer their efforts to new but related targets.[2] Installing metal detectors in airports, for

---

[1] Todd Sandler and Harvey E. Lapan, "The Calculus of Dissent: An Analysis of Terrorists' Choice of Targets," *Synthese* 76 (1988), pp. 245-261.

[2] Walter Enders, Todd Sandler and Joe Cauley, "UN Conventions, Technology and Retaliation in the Fight Against Terrorism: An Econometric Evaluation," *Terrorism and Political Violence*, 2 (1990), pp. 83-105. Further support for the substitution effect is presented in Walter Enders and Todd Sandler, "Transnational Terrorism in the Post-Cold War Era," *International Studies Quarterly*, 43 (1999), pp. 145-167. See also Jon Cauley and Eric Iksoon Im, "Intervention Policy Analysis of Skyjackings and Other Terrorist Incidents," *AEA Papers and Proceedings*, 78 (1988), pp. 27-31.

example, apparently led to a decrease in hijackings but to an increase in other forms of hostage seizures, such as kidnappings, and in assassinations. Thus as a primary set of targets is defended or hardened, terrorists move to softer and easier targets that are more accessible and less risky. For example, when governments learned to counter hijackings, terrorists responded with bombs concealed on board aircraft.

Moreover, once campaigns of terrorism gain momentum, the organization faces internal pressures that encourage activism and escalation via the expansion of targets. The expectations of constituents, including demands for revenge, and frustration among younger cadres are two sources of pressure. If the organization has no purpose other than violence, then continuing to act is the price of continuing to exist. The group will be extremely risk-prone rather than risk-averse.

How, then, do campaigns of terrorism come to an end? And what is the contribution of government policy to the decline of terrorism? Although improved security measures have undoubtedly played a role in suppressing terrorism, sometimes government actions either deflect terrorism onto new targets or stimulate retaliation. Studies of how terrorism ends point to additional factors such as the terrorists' perception of the loss of popular support, demoralization within the organization, and the conclusion on the part of leaders that terrorism has served its purpose and is no longer useful.[3] A deliberate decision to end terrorism typically requires strong leaders who can control a rebellious rank-and-file that wishes to continue.

The motives for suicide terrorism do not appear to differ significantly from the general motives for terrorism, which include revenge, retaliation, and provocation of government over-reaction.

---

[3] See Martha Crenshaw, "Why Violence is Rejected or Renounced: A Case Study of Oppositional Terrorism," in *The Natural History of Peace*, ed. Tom Gregor. (Nashville, TN: Vanderbilt University Press, 1996.)

These objectives may be tactical goals in the end of disrupting peace processes or acquiring political recognition and status. Although terrorism is often described in terms of pure emotionalism or "fanaticism," its instrumental or strategic dimensions should not be overlooked. Furthermore, an opposition movement is often compelled to avenge perceived injustices in order to maintain internal loyalty and cohesion as well as popular support.

The most distinctive characteristic of suicide terrorism, however, appears to be the motive of individual self-sacrifice and martyrdom. It is this willingness to die that makes it appear irrational to many observers. The phenomenon cannot be explained exclusively as the most efficient way of eluding the government's defenses in order to gain access to desirable targets, although this practical consideration is a factor. The individual terrorist's willingness to face not just high risk but certain death requires a psycho-cultural explanation.

One way of looking at this problem is to consider the alternatives, if an individual or group wishes to make a political point and achieve martyrdom. Political suicide as a form of protest is a well-known phenomenon. It represents an attempt to exert power over government policy. In 1936, for example, Stefan Lux shot himself on the floor of the League of Nations to protest against Britain's failure to act against Germany. Self-immolations are another form of individual protest. During the Vietnam War, for example, Buddhist monks set fire to themselves to protest the regime in South Vietnam, which led to imitation elsewhere.

Hunger strikes are somewhat different, in that hunger strikers in effect take themselves hostage. If the government concedes to their demands they can live. Death is not necessary for success, although it is the second-best choice if the government will not give in, because it dramatizes the government's heartlessness and the individual's conviction. However, hunger strikes resemble suicide terrorism in the premium they place on martyrdom, which clearly has a cultural base. Unless martyrdom were valued by society or at least by a subculture, individuals would not seek it. In Ireland, hunger strikes, such as that organized by the IRA in 1981 when ten militants died, are based on a long heritage of traditions of both self-sacrifice and militant republicanism.[4] Martyrs have a high value as propaganda. Furthermore, the individual's belief that he glorifies both himself and the cause is based on a powerful redemptive myth. Salvation is attained through sacrifice. The cult of self-sacrifice, which preceded and went beyond Irish republicanism, had its roots in 18th and 19th century romanticism and the glorification of the heroic individual. It could be seen as a rejection of modernity.

The functions of martyrdom for a resistance movement are varied. It demonstrates the legitimacy and authenticity of the cause, for example. The truth of the cause is established by the individual's willingness to sacrifice everything in its behalf. The martyr self-consciously creates a model for future emulation and inspiration. He expects to impress an audience and to be remembered. For someone whose life otherwise has little significance, transcendent fame can be a powerful motive. The act also flatters all who follow, since they are identified with the heroism and glory of the act of self-sacrifice. The individual, whose identity might otherwise fade into obscurity, has now established a legend for all time. As in suicide bombings, anonymity is rejected.

When one adds these properties to the terrorist equation, the result is a powerful combination. Consider the Russian revolutionaries of the late 19th century. In many cases individual terrorists (as they proudly called themselves) knew that in order to be reasonably certain of hitting their targets they would have to die with their bombs. Some who survived the explosions but were captured subsequently refused offers of clemency in order to

---

[4] These remarks are based on George Sweeney, "Irish Hunger Strikes and the Cult of Self-Sacrifice," Journal of Contemporary History, Vol. 28 (1993), pp. 421-37. The suffragist movement in England also practiced hunger strikes.

sacrifice their lives for the cause. The aura of nobility that terrorism inspired led Albert Camus to title his play "Les Justes," or in English translation "The Just Assassins." To sacrifice oneself was a moral justification for terrorism. Camus criticized later terrorists, such as the FLN during the Algerian war, for their unwillingness to sacrifice themselves as well as for the indiscriminate or unlimited nature of their anti-European violence. This stance earned Camus the enmity of the Left, including notably Jean Paul Sartre. (Nevertheless, it should be noted although the original Russian terrorists were selective in their targeting, not aiming for the civilian population in general, bystanders were frequently killed.)

A fictional example from the same time period is the character of the professor in Joseph Conrad's *The Secret Agent*. An anarchist, he carries a bomb in his pocket at all times, with the detonator cord in his hand. He is said to plan to use it if the police try to arrest him. When asked if he would really carry out the threat, he responds that his willingness does not matter. What matters is that the police believe that he will do so.

Another historical example has even more immediate relevance to the present. Three separate Muslim communities in Asia during the colonial period, from the mid-18th century well into the 20th, practiced suicide attacks.[5] Although their violence did not involve bombings, otherwise it sounds strikingly familiar. As Stephen Dale concludes, "The suicidal attacks by Muslims in Asia represent a premodern form of terrorism, and by studying them it is possible to appreciate why many Muslims regard the recent terrorist attacks in the Middle East as only a more politicized variant of a type of anticolonial resistance that long antedates the twentieth century."[6]

The terrorists were a minority of the Muslim community, which was an Islamic subculture along the coastal areas of the Indian Ocean region, but their actions generated great fear among

---

[5] Stephen F. Dale, "Religious Suicide in Islamic Asia: Anticolonial Terrorism in India, Indonesia, and the Philippines," *Journal of Conflict Resolution*, Vol. 32, No. 1 (March, 1988), pp. 37-59.

[6] Ibid., p. 39.

Europeans. The activists were often young and almost always poor, and their resistance was marginal to the outcome of the conflict against colonial rule. Terrorism occurred at periods of desperation, when militant Muslims realized that resistance to the Europeans could not succeed. Individual assaults were intended to defend the integrity of the Muslim community as much as to intimidate Europeans or local Christians. The terrorists felt that they had embarked on a "private jihad." A sense of religious duty and a desire to acquire individual merit inspired their actions. Common factors in the suicidal jihads included heroic literatures (including epics, songs, and poems as well as legal and theological treatises) that glorified martyrdom as well as specific rituals performed prior to carrying out the attacks. Epic narratives in particular memorialized their sacrifice and inspired imitation.

The martyrs were widely revered in Muslim society. In some cases, the individual who changed his mind about carrying out an attack was scorned as a "half-martyr."[7] Religious authorities sanctioned their acts, although it is important to recognize that the structure of the religious establishment was not centralized or hierarchical. Undoubtedly suicidal jihads had legitimacy in the Muslim community.

How did this wave of terrorism come to an end? Dale argues that terrorism occurred only after military resistance to colonialism had failed, and that it was abandoned when new political opportunities opened up (in some cases as late as the 1920s). When it was possible to form nationalist political organizations with access to political power, terrorism seemed irrelevant and anachronistic. Terrorism was as much instrumental as emotional. Dale notes, however, that when terrorism becomes a cultural norm, its original purpose can be forgotten or perverted. Later attacks may have only a weak connection to the conditions or feelings that initially inspired violence.[8]

---

[7] Ibid., p. 52.

[8] Ibid., pp. 56-57.

In conclusion, then, the suicide terrorism of the 1980's and 1990's is not unusual in terms of the history of terrorism. The power of the bomb is linked to the power of martyrdom. Self-sacrifice is a way of legitimizing a cause, inspiring imitation, and promising individual glory. The concept of self-sacrifice is culturally rooted, in the sense that it can be valued by specific national or religious communities. However, it is not specific to any given culture.

Trends in Contemporary International Terrorism

Ely Karmon

Senior research scholar, ICT.

This paper is an assessment of the main characteristics of international terrorism in the last decade and an evaluation of the main trends for the near future. The dramatic events and changes in the international arena in the 1980's and 1990's have proven that it is unrealistic and dangerous to voice evaluations and predictions for the long term.

Assessment of the main trends

My first argument will be that international terrorism in the 1990's has not changed as dramatically as the media or some researchers sometimes affirm it.

One way of making this argument could be by referring to the research of the Rand Corporation, published lately under the significant title "Countering the New Terrorism." This is indeed the most comprehensive, up-to date and serious research of this last decade on the subject of terrorism, and it was long overdue.[9] However, although most of the data and the analysis in the book are accurate and significant, some of the conclusions concerning the characteristics of the "new" terrorism and its trends, as presented by Bruce Hoffman, do not match with the history of international terrorist activity in the 1970's and 1980's.[10]

According to many researches, including those of RAND and the Patterns of Global Terrorism reports issued annually by the

---

[9] See Ian O. Lesser, Bruce Hoffman, John Arquilla, David F. Ronfeldt, Michele Zanini, Brian Michael Jenkins, *Countering the New Terrorism*, Published by RAND 1999 (http://www.rand.org/publications/MR/MR989/MR989.pdf/)

[10] Ibid. Bruce Hoffman, Chapter Two: "Terrorism Trends and Prospects."

U.S. State Department, the international terrorism of the second half of the 1990's has diminished in quantity of incidents while the quality of the attacks and their lethality has increased dramatically.[11] The subject of lethality is indeed very important, and will lead us to discuss later the possible use by terrorists of what is called in the accepted terminology "Weapons of Mass Destruction" (WMD).

But if we look back to the 1970's and 1980's we should remember many major terrorist attacks against civilian airplanes by sophisticated barometer or time bombs. Swissair, Austrian Airlines, Air India, El Al, TWA, Pan Am (in Honolulu and not at Lockerbie) and other airlines suffered greatly from such attacks, and fortunately many more were foiled by the security services or by sheer luck. At the beginning of the 1980's, one small Palestinian group, the 15 May Organization, had 12 bomb-suitcases ready to explode on American planes; and in 1988 the PFLP - General Command (of Ahmed Jibril) had in Germany several radio-bombs to be used in attacks against planes.[12]

---

[11] See *Patterns of Global Terrorism,* United States Department of State, (http://www.state.gov/www/ global/ terrorism/ 1999report/1999index.html).

[12] On February 21, 1978, the Swissair flight from Zurich to Lod airport in Israel exploded in air. 38 passengers and 9 crew perished The same day a barometer bomb exploded on an Austrian Airlines' flight from Frankfurt to Vienna with 38 people on board, but the plane landed safely. The PFLP – General Command was responsible for these attacks. See Mickolus, *Transnational Terrorism: A chronology of events, 1968-1979* (London: Aldwych Press, 1980), pp. 159-160. On August 11, 1982, an explosive device went off under the passenger seat of Toro Ozawa, 16, who was flying on a Pan American World Airways B-747 with 284 others from Tokyo to Honolulu. The blast killed him, wounded 16 others, and blew a 12" X 36" hole in the passenger cabin's floor. On August 25, 1982 a book-sized bomb was found under a seat on board a Pan Am flight from Miami. Police noted its apparent similarity to a bomb that had exploded under a seat on a Pan Am jet from Japan earlier in the month. On April 2, 1986, a bomb exploded in seat 10-F of TWA flight 840, enroute from Rome to Athens with 114 passengers and 7 crew.

Among the reasons given for the increased lethality of terrorist attacks is the appearance of new terrorist organizations with more amorphous religious and millenarian aims, organizations with less clear nationalist or ideological motivations.

But again, looking back to the 1980's, the two bombings of the American embassy in Beirut in 1983 and the suicide bombings against the American Marines and the French troops' headquarters in Beirut in 1984 which caused hundred of casualties were also the result of attacks by so called amorphous religious organizations— as the Hizballah at that time was seen, a kind of mysterious umbrella organization known from its telephone statements as Islamic Jihad.

It is true that the weight of the religious movements and groups responsible for terrorist activities has greatly increased in the 1990's and that this has influenced the new tactics and patterns of terrorism. One of the reasons for this change is the neutralization by the security forces, or the extinction as a result of the crumbling of the communist block, of ideological groups and organizations of the extreme left in Western Europe and South America.

The radicalization of religious groups is very clear in the Muslim world and the assassination of Israel's late Prime Minister Itzhak Rabin shows that this trend involves radical Jewish groups as well. It is less obvious in the Christian world, although some of

---

Four passengers were sucked out of the plane, which finally landed safely. The two August 1982 bomb attacks were perpetrated by the 15 May Faction, a plinter-group of the PFLP. The TWA attack was attributed to the Fatah Special Operations Group's intelligence and security apparatus, headed by Abdullah Abd al-Hamid Labib, alias Colonel Hawari. He reportedly had used Palestinian terrorists who previously belonged to the May 15 Organization. See Edward Mickolus, *International Terrorism in the 1980's. A chronology of events* (Ames: Yowa State University Press, 1989). In the 1970's and the beginning of 1980's there were at least three or four cases of Israeli El Al airplanes whose explosion could have caused hundreds of casualties if the attacks had not been foiled or aborted by technical failures.

the radical right-wing terrorists, especially in the United States, are also influenced by religious motivations.[13]

One of the main strategic modes of operation used by such organizations has been suicide terrorism, not only in Lebanon and Israel, but also in Turkey, by the Kurdistan Workers Party (PKK), in Sri Lanka by The Liberation Tigers of Tamil Eelam (LTTE), and in India by Tamil terrorists. It is strategic because it has huge political repercussions, like the disruption of the political process between Israel and the Palestinian Authority in 1995-1996 or the assassination of the Prime Minister Rajib Ghandi in India, and until now there is no operational answer to it.

Looking at the second half of the 1990's, we can see two conflicting trends in international terrorism:

On the one hand there is indeed a trend of radicalization. But the center of gravity of this intense activity has moved from parts of the Middle East and Europe to Afghanistan and Pakistan, the Caucasus and Central Asia. This is a result of the dismembering of the Soviet empire, the aftermath of the Afghanistan war against the Soviets and the political instability in Afghanistan and Pakistan.[14] These two last countries, Afghanistan and Pakistan, have replaced Lebanon as hotbeds of terrorist organizations and playgrounds for the training of groups and individuals from Muslim and non-Muslim countries.

In the Middle Eastern arena, it should be noted that terrorism has had major negative strategic consequences: The suicide terrorism of Hamas and the Palestinian Islamic Jihad has been responsible for the interruption of the negotiating process between Israel and the Palestinian Authority; Hizballah's terrorism and guerrilla activity has furthered not only this organization's goal of destroying Israel, but also Iran's strategic regional interests and Syria's needs in its negotiations with Israel.

---

[13] For a description of this trend see Gilles Keppel, *The Revenge of God: The Resurgence of Islam, Christianity and Judaism in the Modern World* (London: Polity Press, 1995).

[14] See also *Patterns of Global Terrorism* 1999.

As a consequence of this trend, the major international activity has been staged this decade by the radical Islamist organizations. Osama bin-Ladin, his al-Qaeda organization and the World Islamic Front for the Struggle against Jews and Crusaders he created has grown on this background.

On the other hand, it is important to stress that we witness a counter-current—the shift to the political process and negotiation by important organizations as a means to achieve their strategic goals. This is true for the Irish Republican Army (IRA) in Northern Ireland, the PKK in Turkey, and the Fuerzas Armadas Revolucionarias de Columbia (FARC) in Colombia; but also for the Front Islamique du Salut (FIS) in Algeria and the al-Jihad and Gama'at al-Islamyya in Egypt. It is important to be attentive to this trend, to understand the motivations behind it and to learn the mechanisms that can be used on other fronts.

This trend is probably the result of the failure of armed struggle to bring the vital strategic results expected by the organizations involved, and the example they saw in the achievements of the PLO through negotiation and the political process. But as in the case of the political process between Israel and the Palestinians, there are splits, difficulties, and crises in all the negotiating processes attempted by these organizations.

It is of note that, contrary to many expectations, the wars in Bosnia and Kosovo have not produced significant terrorist activities. The support that the democratic countries, under the leadership of the United States, have given to the Muslim populations of these two countries has proven to many Muslims around the world that the West is not the demonized enemy described by the radical Islamists, and thus prevented the use of this front by radicals like Osama bin-Ladin.

Terrorism of the far-right has also changed location: It developed in Europe at the end of the 1980's and beginning of the 1990's but emerged as a greater threat in the United States later in the decade. The Oklahoma City bombing has proven that this indiscriminate terrorism, using the new "leaderless" strategy, can be as lethal as radical religious terrorism.

A trend of the second half of the 1990's has been the diminution of state sponsorship of terrorism. The main states sponsoring terrorism—Libya, Syria, Iraq, North Korea, and even Iran (after the 1997 election of reformist President Khatami)—have diminished substantially their involvement in international terrorism, especially after the Gulf War. This was mainly the result of the political and economic pressure exerted by the United States and the international community. The major terrorist attacks of the 1990's—the Oklahoma City and New York World Trade Center bombings—had nothing to do with state sponsorship; neither did the Kenya and Tanzania American embassy bombings, although for these last attacks Afghanistan could be held indirectly responsible.

The only new major changes in the terrorism of the 1990's have been the appearance of cults in the arena of terrorism and the breaking of the taboo in the use of non-conventional terrorism, which is in itself connected to the activity of one cult, the now famous Japanese Aum Shinrikyo.

The threat of millenarian and apocalyptic groups exists, although in this field security and intelligence agencies are very much in the dark in identifying potential terrorists because of political, moral and legal constraints. For instance, the Israeli Police have great difficulties in deciding who is a crazy Christian millenarian hiding in the grottos of the Judean desert or a member of a potentially dangerous cult like the American Concerned Christians, who could commit suicide terrorism on the Temple Mount and thus trigger a war of religion.

Some comments on the Aum Shinrikyo cult, the most remarkable example in this category, could clarify some problems and doubts concerning cult. Aum can be considered not only as an apocalyptic cult, but as a religious/ideological organization: it had a clear anti-American, anti-Western and anti-Semitic ideology, a political and strategic plan for taking power in Japan (it even ran as a party in the general elections) and it had an organizational pattern similar to a government. What characterizes it most is the kind of dictatorship of the guru and his total influence on his followers, which is found in many cults and new-religion groups. It is interesting to note that the "Marxist-Leninist" Japanese Red Army of the 1970's was no less a dictatorship than Aum—on a smaller scale—and similarly violent to its members and to the innocent people around it.

In the framework of the subject that interests this conference, suicide terrorism, some remarks concerning the operational activity of Aum Shinrikyo are instructive.

Non-conventional terrorism—that is, chemical, biological, radiological and nuclear terrorism—implies perhaps a kind of suicide aspect, as it could in most cases clearly endanger the perpetrators of the attacks themselves. The Aum leadership and the activists in the operational field were aware of this, and, contrary to what could be expected of an apocalyptic cult, they decided to protect themselves from the lethal effects of the chemical weapons they produced and later used.[15]

Not only did they purchase sophisticated devices for the protection of their personnel, create a medical team and a hospital specialized in treating wounds resulting from the production of chemical weapons; but they also took every technical and operational precaution in order not to endanger their operatives. The attack in the Tokyo subway in March 1995 caused only a limited number of casualties because it had been decided to dilute the Sarin content of the packages used, in order to secure the lives of the operational team and not of the public. This was in fact a lesson Aum operatives had learned from the previous attack they staged in Matsumoto in 1994, during which the team used almost lost their lives.

Most likely, one of the reasons Aum Shinrikyo abandoned its earlier plan to produce biological weapons was the conclusion that

---

[15] For an account of Aum Shinrinkyo activities see D.W. Brackett, *Holy Terror: Armageddon in Tokyo* (New York, 1996) and Richard Falkenrath, Robert Newman & Bradley Thayer, *America's Achilles' Heel* (Cambridge, Mass., 1998), pp. 19-26.

they could not control the dissemination of the viruses involved, and therefore would endanger themselves.

Another suicidal aspect in the use of non-conventional terrorism is the fact that the successful use by an organization of chemical or biological terrorism could produce such a severe military reaction by the country attacked as to endanger the life of a large fraction of the constituent population that this organization claims to represent. It would in fact amount to a collective suicide attack. For this reason it is obvious that any serious organization takes into account this danger, and this could be one explanation for the small number of incidents and alerts registered until today in the field of non-conventional terrorism.

Weapons of Mass Destruction or Non-conventional Terrorism

This brings us to the overall evaluation of the threat represented by non-conventional terrorism. This evaluation is based on a year-long research project on the subject of non-conventional terrorism led by the ICT.

ICT researchers collected publicly available reports of incidents and built a database of non-conventional terrorist attacks, although the very definition of non-conventional terrorism and the significance of each incident is a matter of controversy among researchers. This is not a complete or exhaustive database, but it surely includes most of the known and significant ones—292 incidents in all. The incidents were classified by the period of occurrence (divided into three decades), the continent and country of occurrence, and by their degree of severity.

Categories and period of occurrence (see annex I)

From the analysis of all 292 incidents of non-conventional terrorism, it results that the number of incidents of *nuclear terrorism* (167 in all) have sharply declined over the past three decades: from 120 incidents during the 1970's to only 15 in the 1990's. In contrast, incidents of *chemical* and *biological terrorism* (84 and 41 respectively) are showing a gradual but steady rise. In the 1970's there were 14 incidents of chemical terrorism and 10 incidents of biological terrorism; in the 1980's there were 34 incidents of chemical terrorism and 13 incidents of biological terrorism; whereas in the 1990's there are 36 reported incidents of chemical terrorism and 18 incidents of biological terrorism.

It is clear from Annex I that most of the terrorism involving nuclear targets happened in the 1970's and diminished dramatically in the next two decades. What is the reason for this astonishing trend?

It should be stressed that these actions were due mainly to the activity of extremist left-wing organizations, which opposed American and Western nuclear armament and deployment of nuclear missiles, especially in Europe. With the disintegration of the anti-nuclear movement in the middle of the 1980's and parallel with the elimination of the violent extremist leftist groups in Europe and the fall of the Soviet Union (which had a strategic interest in supporting the anti-nuclear movement), violent anti-nuclear activity almost disappeared.

As to chemical and biological terrorism, it has clearly developed in the 1980's and 1990's, after the war between Iraq and Iran; and again after the Gulf War of the U.S.-led coalition against Iraq.

The indiscriminate use of chemical weapons by the Iraqis and the fear that the Gulf War would provoke a large chemical-biological conflict and a wave of non-conventional terrorism brought about the feeling that this kind of terrorism was inevitable. The attacks perpetrated by the Japanese Aum Shinrikyo cult in March 1995 were a surprise only because of where they happened and the magnitude of the infrastructure at the disposal of the organization. Today it is known that the Gulf War influenced the decision by Aum's leader, Soho Asahara, to produce and use chemical and biological weapons.

Between the two types of attack, chemical terrorism has a clear advantage over biological, not only in the number of incidents involved but also in their seriousness and lethality.

Incidents by degree of severity (see Annex II)

The incidents were classified into seven categories according to their degree of severity. From the table in Annex II it results that the great majority of incidents were nuclear terrorism, but of these, most were threats (98) or actions against facilities (43), and only few involved real attacks or attempts of attacks (two and two respectively). Terrorists have not attacked "live" nuclear facilities, stolen nuclear weapons or weapons-grade nuclear materials, nor even committed credible nuclear hoaxes—except perhaps the Chechen threat to use radiological materials in Moscow in 1995.

It should be noted that a considerable number of threats or incidents involving the terrorist use of chemical agents have been reported in the open literature, but the majority of these were characterized as isolated, not serious or significant, not on a large scale, and even inept, except the Aum Shinrikyo attack in March 1995 in the Tokyo subway stations. Few terrorist groups have attempted to acquire biological agents, and even fewer have actually attempted to use the agents. The number of known victims (no known fatalities) from bio-terrorist incidents is limited to the 751 people who became sick during the 1984 Rajeeshnee cult attacks in a restaurant in Oregon, U.S.A.

Incidents according to location (see Annex III)

Almost 55% of the incidents occurred in the United States. Of those: 75% were incidents of nuclear terrorism, 14% incidents of chemical terrorism and 11% incidents of biological terrorism.

Nearly 28% of the incidents have occurred in Europe, of which 53% were incidents of nuclear terrorism, 31% incidents of chemical terrorism, and only 16% incidents of biological terrorism.

The incidents that took place in the Middle East represent only 4% of the total; of those, 10 out of 12 were incidents of chemical terrorism and 2 were of bio-terrorism. However, it should be noted that Middle Eastern countries (Egypt, Iraq, Iran and possibly Sudan) have made relatively massive use of chemical weapons. 10.5% of the incidents have occurred in Asia and some 1% each took place in South America and Africa.

These findings may indicate that non-conventional terrorism is not common where conventional terrorism is a major factor, such as the Middle East and South America.

By contrast, the existing data shows that the developed, industrial world (U.S., Europe and Japan) was the main ground for non-conventional terrorism, the United States leading the targeted countries.

This means, in our opinion, that an advanced industrial-technological infrastructure is necessary for the development of a non-conventional capability by a terrorist organization. It should be noted also that the facilities targeted (nuclear or chemical plants, military weapons, etc.) are also usually found in these countries.

In this sense, the U.S.A is not only the most technologically advanced and developed country in the world, but is also, ideologically, the super-power leader of the Western democratic camp during the Cold War and the only super-power left in the era of the "New World [dis] Order." Therefore, it was and is the main target for terrorist attacks, including non-conventional ones. This is also the reason why the American administration considers WMD terrorism as the main threat to its security in the 21st century.

Conclusion

The ICT research examined non-conventional terrorism from two perspectives: desire and capability. First, we identified motivations, objectives, and the inclination of terrorist groups to expand their options and utilize non-conventional terrorism. The second part analyzed the technical barriers facing terrorist groups that seek to develop their own chemical, biological, radiological and nuclear weapons. We distinguish two major threats - limited and extreme non-conventional attacks.

"Limited" non-conventional attacks in some sense parallel established terrorist doctrine. We concluded that terrorist organizations are capable of perpetrating indiscriminate attacks involving perhaps hundreds of casualties in order to influence psychologically and politically public opinion and governments and thus achieve their strategic goals.

"Extreme" attacks represent a significant departure from current thinking and an attempt completely to change current reality. As most terrorist groups employ a rational cost-benefit evaluation and recognize that some costs may be prohibitively high, we find that such attacks are unlikely and inconsistent with present terrorist thinking. Moreover, the existing organizations and groups, because of the complex problems of dissemination and control of non-conventional agents, are not technologically capable of extermination attacks involving annihilation or contamination of whole towns or regions

We found that chemical weapons are somewhat easier to develop (although they represent a significant challenge to most terrorist groups), biological ones more difficult but potentially far more lethal, and nuclear weapons practically impossible. Moreover, we found that while chemical weapons are probably the easiest to develop, they are not likely to be more effective in terrorist hands than high explosives.

This new view replaces exaggerated assessments of terrorist capability with a more realistic perspective. It does not, however, address the important case of a country providing chemical, biological or nuclear weapons to sponsored organizations. That such transfers have not occurred is encouraging, but is not a guarantee for the future.

It should be stressed, however, that the potential threat of non-conventional terrorism is real and even the perpetration of relatively minor or limited lethal attacks could have enormous psychological, political and social consequences for the countries involved and for international society.

New trends and threats

The emerging radical Sunni terrorism

As a result of the victory of the Afghanis and their Arab allies over the Soviet Union, the Gulf War, the increased military American and Western presence in Saudi Arabia and the Gulf area, and the consequences of the Western military activity against Iraq, the already existing Sunni radicalism has developed into the main terrorist threat in the region.

The victory of the extremist religious Taliban in the internal struggle in Afghanistan and the increased instability and radicalization of the Pakistani Islamist movements and of the regime itself, have given to these Sunni movements and groups the necessary territory to organize, train, make sorties and take refuge in case of necessity. The investigations following the bombing of the World Trade Center and the assassination of CIA officers in Washington have highlighted these trends.

The gray zones and new battle zones

And here lies the next threat, the existence and expansion of the so-called gray zones: countries and territories under control of anarchic fighting groups without the presence of moderating Western or international forces. Somalia, Chechnya, Central Africa and parts of Afghanistan and Pakistan have become the exclusive territories of such uncontrollable and violent forces. Bin-Ladin and his allies, like the splinter groups of Egyptian Islamists, can find refuge or a battle ground for their followers in these faraway corners of the world.

This trend is enhanced by the appearance of new battle zones for the Islamist radicals: Russia, the Central Asian Muslim republics, and possibly parts of Indonesia in the near future.

Sunni - Shia clash

This is a relatively new phenomenon, which has received little attention from researchers and the media, but is starting to be documented by Sunni radical publications and websites: the growing antagonism between radical Sunni and radical Shi'a groups and countries.

The background to this development is the struggle by terrorist methods between majority Sunni and minority Shi'a movements in Pakistan, the religious and social oppression of Sunnis in Iran, the strategic and ideological clash between Shi'a Iran and Sunni Afghanistan, and activity of extremist Sunni groups in Lebanon.

This trend may develop and influence future events in the Middle East and the rest of the Muslim world.

Growing international cooperation

However, there is also an optimistic trend in the international arena of the late 1990's. During the last decade, and more so during the last two to three years, we have witnessed a growing readiness and interest on the part of more countries to cooperate in the fight against terrorism, on the local, regional and global arena.

The successful cooperation in the fight against the radical Hamas and the Palestinian Islamic Jihad between the security forces of Israel and the Palestinian Authority is only one example of local cooperation. The regional agreement reached by the countries of the Arab League to fight radical Islamic movements jointly has already had positive effects for Egypt's fight against al-Jihad and Gama'at Islamiya.

The United Nations itself is more and more involved in this battle: the embargo on Libya and the opening of the trial in the Lockerbie affair, or the sanctions against Afghanistan for the extradition of Osama bin-Ladin, would not have been possible some years ago. And who would have dreamed that the UN would create its own Terrorism Prevention Branch, as part of the larger Office for Drug Control and Crime Prevention in Vienna?

This international cooperation has resulted also in the decrease in state sponsorship of international terrorism. Today only Iran, Syria, and Afghanistan can be considered real sponsors or supporters of terrorist organizations; and even they are constrained to more caution and secrecy in their activity than they exercised in the past.

Hopefully this trend will prevail, although as a whole it is clear that international and internal terrorism will remain a major element in the lives of our countries and in the global arena in the next decade.

Annex I

Table of Incidents by Categories
and Period of Occurrence

Period	Number of incidents			
	Nuclear	Chemical	Biological	Total
1970-1979	120	14	10	144
1980-1989	32	34	13	79
1990-1998	15	36	18	69
Total	167	84	41	292

Annex II

Table of Incidents by Degree of Severity

Severity	Number of Incidents			
	Nuclear	Chemical	Biological	Total
Threats to Use WMD	10	28	13	51
Threats Against WMD Facilities	98	-	-	98
Attempts to Acquire WMD	11	6	7	24
Possession of WMD	1	8	6	15
Attempted Use of WMD	2	4	10	16
Action Against Facilities of WMD	43	3	-	46
Actual Use of WMD	2	35	5	42
Total	167	84	41	292

Annex III

Diagram of Incidents by Location

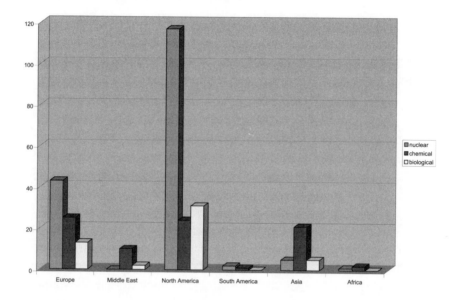

International Terrorism and International Cooperation

Frank Anderson

Former Head of the Near East Division, Central Intelligence Agency, U.S.A.

I must begin by providing advance apologies for what I suspect will be at least some disappointment in the content of the remarks that follow. Given the expertise that is assembled here, it is highly unlikely that I will be providing any new information. Given the complexity and intractability of the issue we are here to consider, I do not expect to be able to provide any suggestions for dealing with terrorism that have not already occurred to the experts gathered here.

Finally, I must apologize to anyone who expects to learn any secrets or receive any official insights from me. Given my background, it is unavoidable that I will bring the focus and, perhaps, bias of a former American Intelligence officer to this discussion. Before going on, however, I need to emphasize the word "former" and to specify that I am speaking as a private citizen. Nothing I am about to say represents an official viewpoint or includes non-public information.

I will, nevertheless, attempt, from the point of view of a former practitioner who maintains an active amateur interest in the subject, to provide a brief overview of the reasons international cooperation is necessary, the ways in which it takes place, and some comments on the current environment in which it takes place.

Earlier this month, America's Director of Central Intelligence, George Tenet, testified before the U.S. Senate's Select Committee on Intelligence on "The Worldwide Threat in 2000: Global Realities of Our National Security."

He opened the section of his remarks on terrorism by noting that "since July 1998, working with foreign governments worldwide, we have helped to render more that two dozen terrorists to justice…These renditions have shattered terrorist cells and networks, thwarted terrorist plans, and in some cases even prevented attacks from occurring."

The period 1998-2000 is, of course, not the first in which a senior U.S. official could have reported success in breaking up terrorist organizations, disrupting their plans and preventing attacks. It was certainly not unusual that remarks on such successes would include the clause, "working with foreign governments worldwide." By its nature, terrorism often, probably most often, can only be countered through international cooperation.

Terrorism can (as it is usually intended to do) drive or keep nations apart. It is, on the other hand, an issue on which nations can (and frequently, even regularly do) focus and/or base significant cooperation.

The issues which motivate international terrorism, the people who commit international terrorist acts, the weapons, the money, almost always come from or, at least, move among multiple countries.

The causes and countermeasures of terrorism are, to a great extent, integral to, or at the very least, affected by the broader realm of international affairs.

Certainly, international cooperation against terrorism is tied to the overall relationship between nations. International terrorism both emerges from and impacts international and/or sectarian conflicts such as the Arab-Israeli conflict, and the enduring and intractable dispute between India and Pakistan. Working against the associated terrorism necessarily involves the broader effort to address the core issues which underlie these conflicts. An effective effort against terrorism must be part of an effective foreign policy.

On more operational levels, the need for international cooperation and the inevitability of international complications are clear to even a casual observer of the various elements of any nation's effort against terrorism. Few, if any, of the actions nations take to counter terrorism are uncomplicated by international concerns.

Simple security measures impact on relations between nations. The fortress-like buildings that are now America's and other nations' embassies isolate the diplomats who work in those buildings from the people with whom they must interact to do their work effectively. The screening of air travelers has at least some negative impact on the travelers' interest in international business and tourism. The millenium terrorism warnings which the U.S. and other governments gave to their citizens late last year had a serious negative impact on tourism here, in Jordan, and in the rest of the Middle East.

Beyond political and diplomatic efforts to find solutions or amelioration to the conflicts from which much international terrorism arises, diplomacy plays an important and necessary role in countering terrorism. Diplomatic effort is required to build coalitions against terrorism and to ostracize terrorists and those who support them. Diplomacy can and often does play an important role in efforts to deny capabilities to terrorists and to states that sponsor them. Diplomacy is needed to create and sustain export-control regimes and financial controls which are important, albeit surprisingly difficult and costly, measures to limit the flow of arms and cash to terrorist organizations.

Paradoxically, the democratic practices and human rights concerns of target nations often seriously complicate international efforts to deal with the international terrorist groups that wish, and frequently do them harm. Asylum provisions in the legal systems of most democracies now frequently result in situations in which individuals and groups who advocate or even participate in terrorist support against friendly nations are able to do so without fear of return to and prosecution in their home countries.

In my view, military response to terrorism has recently been effective, but problematic. Nevertheless, it certainly impacts significantly upon relations between the acting nation and the target. It also inevitably involves other difficult interactions with nations who disagree with the action, as it always involves unintended or, at least, unwelcome effects on many people and interests beyond the intended targets. Military forces are organized, equipped and trained to destroy other military forces. Using them for other purposes always involves a costly and difficult process of shoving a square peg into a round hole.

Law-enforcement and intelligence cooperation across national frontiers against terrorism is the area with which I have the most familiarity. The factors which compel such cooperation are obvious to intelligence and security professionals, but may not be so apparent to others.

The intelligence services of all of the countries represented here are called upon to contribute to their countries' overall counter-terrorist programs. The remarkable challenges that this poses to any nation's foreign intelligence service are probably not immediately obvious, and may even be counterintuitive to those outside the intelligence and security communities.

U.S. intelligence presence abroad, and the foreign presence of the intelligence services of other nations, is (despite some popular perceptions) relatively small. The information and resources required to deal with terrorism, on the other hand, can only be obtained by much larger forces.

Terrorism, whatever its motivation, is crime. In many, perhaps most, terrorist organizations, crime and relationships with criminals play a part in recruitment, establishing operational infrastructure, and finance. Hence, this usually is an issue best handled by police forces. Only police or internal security services have wide and deep involvement in the societies that they serve and protect (or, in some unfortunate cases, oppress and abuse) and in which the terrorists obtain recruits, resources and assistance. Developing the range of human sources required to deal effectively with the challenge of terrorist organizations requires such deep integration into the societies from which the terrorists arise and is, almost always, simply impossible for a foreign intelligence service, however efficient it might be.

Police and internal security organizations of most nations, on the other hand, lack the ability to collect, analyze and disseminate vast amounts of data which are routinely gathered and handled by the complex and sometimes highly technical, intelligence organizations of the U.S. and other major powers. Sometimes, the U.S. and other nations are able to provide financial and other resources that are unavailable to the smaller, relatively less well-funded, but otherwise highly skilled and effective security organizations of smaller countries.

So, with infrequent exception, effective work against terrorist organizations requires the involvement of the police or internal security organizations of two or more governments, working in conjunction with their own external intelligence organizations and those of other countries.

It is worth noting another important role which intelligence organizations sometimes play in this arena. It is frequently the case that the tangled web of motivations and actions related to international terrorism is difficult to deal with openly. Combinations of nations, which are unable or unwilling to cooperate openly on most or all issues, nevertheless have a strong interest to cooperate on the issue of terrorism. That makes counter-terrorism an issue on which nations which are otherwise enemies can open lines of communication and cooperation. These openings are sensitive and complex, and usually, don't bear exposure well. Intelligence organizations, by their nature, can provide or sustain discreet relations and/or communications between parties that cannot openly meet to discuss counter-terrorist cooperation or conduct early explorations into possible resolutions of the conflicts from which much terrorism emerges.

What is the current environment in which this cooperation takes place, or at least ought to take place? It is, for one thing, complex enough to pose a real challenge to an effort to organize any remarks on 21st century terrorism and counter-terrorism cooperation into anything more integrated than stream-of-consciousness chatter. Terrorism is not new, it's not simple, it's not neat, nor is it neatly categorizable. It is, to steal a term used by Paul Pillar, the Deputy Chief of CIA's Counter-terrorist Center, an "epiphenomenon" of many other and very complex social and political issues. Sometimes it is the organized and disciplined actions of a state engaged in support of declared or undeclared war against another state. Sometimes it is criminal behavior by members of a private or, at least, non-government organization. Sometimes it is a spontaneous act of a deranged individual without rational purpose. Usually, it is a complex combination of more than one such syndrome. That complexity is perhaps more significant today than in recent decades.

The most immediately apparent development in recent years has been a shift from (but, by no means the disappearance of) international terrorism as a tool of foreign policy by states or state sponsored organizations. This has been offset by the increasing (but, by no means, new) involvement in terrorism by non-government groups, individuals and, often, "non-group groups" of individuals who come together for the purpose of committing a terrorist act and then separate.

Much of the trend away from state sponsored terrorism is related to the end of the Cold War. The collapse of the Soviet Union and the general discrediting of the scientific socialist ideologies with which the cause of Soviet Communism was associated (and effective police work in Europe and East Asia) have resulted in the virtual disappearance of groups like the Italian Red Brigades and the German Red Army Faction. Eastern European states, during the Cold War, were prominent supporters of terrorist groups because that support was an integral part of those states' overall support of the foreign policy objectives of the Soviet Bloc. Those states no longer have a motivation to support terrorist organizations, but do have strong motives to interact positively with their former opponents in the West. So, they are no longer in the business of supporting terrorism.

Groups like the Irish Republican Army and Palestinian organizations whose ambitions and motivations are nationalistic, but who previously drew support for terrorist acts from, among others, the states of the former Soviet Bloc, are shifting to political pursuit of their objectives. This is partly because of the loss of superpower support. It is more directly related to increasingly realistic prospects of accomplishment of their nationalist aims through a political process.

The world is certainly safer because of the end of the Cold War. The turn away from support for terrorism by some states and the demise of terrorist groups who killed out of devotion to a scientific socialist ideology are welcome developments. Terrorism is still a tool of statecraft for several states, however. Moreover, the withdrawal from the terrorist scene by many states and state supported organizations has been accompanied by growth in the number and significance of non-state organizations, who in many ways pose more persistent and intractable threats than do governments or government-supported groups.

Not surprisingly, the countries who are still involved in the use or support of terrorism are those whose motivations to support terrorist groups or actions were, at most, only tangentially related to the Cold War.

Iran remains high (probably first) on the list of still-active state sponsors. While participants here might argue over whether violence by Hizballah against Israeli forces in Lebanon is international terrorism, there is no doubt that Iran's continued and recently increased support to Hizballah is a deliberate use of a terrorist organization to advance Iranian national and geopolitical objectives. Similarly, while the exact extent and nature of Iranian involvement in the Khobar Towers bombing is unclear, enough information has gotten out into the public domain to indicate strongly that they were, in at least some way, complicit.

Iran's anti-Western and anti-Israeli motives were, of course, not diminished by the passing away of the superpower rivalry. It remains to be seen whether internal Iranian politics and regional developments might affect Iran's interest in supporting terrorism. In my opinion, there is a real political process going on in Iran where the body politic is truly divided over basic questions on how that society should be organized and ruled. I believe that it is no longer true that "an Iranian moderate is an Iranian who has run out of ammunition." There is a significant political force in Iran that wants more liberty at home and less isolation abroad. That force is and will be motivated to end or reduce Iran's use of and support for terrorism. Still, there are, as yet, no clear indications that internal

Iranian politics are leading the current Iranian regime to drop support for terrorism from its inventory of statecraft tools. Indeed, I believe that there is an internal political incentive for the conservative side in the current Iranian political process to increase Iran's use and/or support of terrorism. The conservative forces in Iran require external enemies to justify their increasingly unpopular controls over the Iranian population. Stirring the international (or, at least, regional) pot through support for terrorist organizations and acts is an effective way to maintain Iran's current inventory of external threats.

Moving closer to this conference site, I personally believe that it is difficult to dismiss the probability that Syrian officials had, at least, guilty knowledge of what seems to have been the involvement of Hizballah elements in Lebanon in providing the explosive device used at Khobar Towers. Syria openly plays host to a number of terrorist groups and clearly seeks to retain support for terrorism as an asset which might be bargained away in the peace process.

Nevertheless, Syria has not left its own clearly complicit fingerprints on an international terrorist act in over a decade. Hafez Al-Assad's regime does have an important interest in efforts toward a peace agreement that would include the return of the Golan Heights to Syria. This does motivate the Syrians to keep out of the business of direct involvement in terrorism. Moreover, Syria's confrontation with Turkey over Syria's provision of support and safe haven to Abdullah Ocalan of the Kurdish Workers' Party showed that the Syrian regime is able to turn overtly on a previous terrorist protégé when the protection of Syrian interests demands that. (I do believe that it would be a mistake to draw a conclusion that Syria's response to Turkish coercion over the Kurdish issue means that they would respond similarly to Israeli coercion within the context of the Arab-Israeli conflict.)

In late 1990 and early 1991, the Iraqis mounted a number of remarkably inept and easily defeated attempts to conduct terrorist operations in response to Desert Shield/Desert Storm. The Iraqi regime has played at least a significant part in an ongoing crime wave in Jordan. For the almost a decade, however, the Iraqi regime's terrorism, for the most part, has been directed at its own suffering population, not the world at large. This absence from the international terrorism scene is, in my view, related solely to lack of capability, rather than lack of motive. So any increase in Iraqi capabilities that might come from the now increasingly popular idea of significant changes in the sanctions regime could very well result in Iraq rejoining the ranks of state sponsors of terrorism. Even without a revival of Iraqi government capabilities to mount or support operations, there might be unwelcome results from reported contacts or relationships between surviving elements of the Abu Nidal Organization in Baghdad and supporters of Osama bin-Ladin's Al-Qa'idah.

Libya has turned over two suspects for trial in the Pan Am Flight 103 case, has deported the members of at least some terrorist groups who had lived for years in Libya, and is working hard at cultivating at least the image of a reformed, former terrorist state that wishes now to enter the community of nations as a responsible member.

Two nations that must be mentioned in this context, India and Pakistan, do not appear on the U.S. Government's list of terrorist supporters. The governments of both states, especially Pakistan in the very recent past, have paid a significant price and have taken significant political risks to cooperate in the struggle against international terrorism. Pakistan also deserves great credit for playing a very significant role and paying a very heavy price in the struggle that brought about the end of the Cold War, and the dismantling of the world's largest complex of state support for terrorism. Nevertheless, India and Pakistan have been in an uninterrupted, although usually undeclared, state of war since their creation as independent states more than 50 years ago. In that conflict both sides have used and/or indulged terrorist groups whose actions and/or ideologies supported each side in this long struggle. Pakistan's involvement with groups fighting what Pakistan regards as India's illegitimate occupation of Kashmir and their support of the Taliban government in Afghanistan, despite the Taliban's persistent protection and support of Osama bin-Ladin, have compromised Pakistan and placed it in danger of being placed on the list of state sponsors of terrorism.

Reference to South Asia is a good point to shift the discussion to a view of the increasing and increasingly lethal involvement in terrorism by individuals and loosely organized groups that are not supported by any government and not motivated by national or irredentist causes. The most prominent current example is Osama bin-Ladin's complex collection of relationships with like-minded individuals and groups across Asia, Africa, Europe, and North America. Although bin-Ladin's support of attacks on Americans in Saudi Arabia is motivated, in part, by a desire to push the U.S. to withdraw its military presence from Saudi Arabia and the terrorist attacks on tourists by Egyptian Islamic Jihad and Gama'a al-Islamiyah are aimed, in part, at damaging the Egyptian economy and, thereby weakening the Egyptian government, these groups are often motivated only by simple hatred and a desire to kill and maim their targets, whether or not there is any other political payoff from their operations.

These groups pose particular problems to those attempting to deal with them. Since they do not rely (or rely less) on states for support, diplomatic engagement with and even military punishment of states is unlikely to deter them. Since they often rely on inspiration, rather than direction, to provoke action by their followers and/or sympathizers, there are no organized communications or support networks which counter-terrorist forces can focus on to identify, disrupt or destroy the organizations. Paradoxically (and frustratingly), in most of the democracies targeted by these groups, the very speech and other expression used to provoke the attacks are vigorously protected by the intended victims.

Reduction in costs and advances in communications technology and, most unfortunately, the technology and lethality of terrorist devices, means that these private groups can afford to operate without the support of states and can inflict death and destruction on a scale that was previously beyond anyone without a state's power and resources. Since they don't try to created disciplined organizations, it is extremely difficult to identify and disrupt them.

The fanatical, now usually religious, ideologies that motivate these groups make them particularly difficult to restrain. Their independence from state sponsors and, often, hatred for all extant forms of government give them immunity from concerns that reactions to their operations could damage their sponsors or governments friendly to them.

Fundamentalist Terrorism

*Session Chairman: Ambassador Michael
Sheehan, Coordinator for Counter-Terrorism,
U.S. Department of State*

Fundamentalist Terrorism:
Introduction

Ambassador Michael Sheehan

Coordinator for Counter-Terrorism, Department of State, U.S.A.

I was asked to make a few opening remarks, and so I will make a couple of introductory remarks about terrorism—particularly suicide terrorism—from the U.S. perspective. The United States, and Israel as well, are targets for terrorists around the world, who use a variety of tactics and espouse a variety of ideologies. Nonetheless, the center stage for us in most recent years has been taken by suicide terrorists emanating primarily from the Middle East and from South Asia, often claiming Islamic religious justification for their acts.

I think it is fair to say that my office devotes a disproportion amount of attention to these groups and the countries that support them. International terrorism by the Middle Eastern groups that plagued us in the '70's and '80's was different in many respects from what we are seeing today. That period was the heyday of high-profile attacks such as airline hijackings, kidnappings, hostage-takings, and indiscriminate shootings and bombings of civilians in public places, such as the international airports in Rome, Athens, and Lod.

The motivations of the most active of these groups in that period, such as the PFLP, DFLP, PLO, Lebanese Armed Revolutionary Faction, Abu Nidal organization and others, were primarily secular, nationalist, often leftist, and almost always anti-Israeli. Terrorists from these groups rarely intended to die and certainly did not plan to become martyrs. During the '80's, a new and in many ways more violent type of terrorism emerged, a terrorism often motivated by religious extremism. The rise of Hizballah in Lebanon, as well as a variety of militant groups claiming to represent fundamentalist values in other countries, marked the beginning of a new and lethal chapter of Middle Eastern terrorism.

These religious terrorist groups introduced us to a terrible new form of violence through the suicide operations that are the subject of this conference. These groups began the practice of recruiting impressionable young men and women, giving them fundamentalist religious indoctrination, and preparing them for martyrdom. Unlike their secular, nationalist, or leftist predecessors, these Islamic terrorists fully intended to die in the course of carrying out an attack. In fact, the terrorist's death became an integral part of the plan of operation.

Terrorists willing to sacrifice their lives during an attack, thereby obviating the need to plan an escape route, presented a unique challenge for our defenses. Moreover, these terrorists have proven to be more fanatical, more determined, and in many ways more unpredictable than their secular predecessors of the 1970's.

The United States immediately became a central target for these terrorists who justified their actions on religious grounds. In 1983 and 1984 Hizballah suicide bombers, backed by Iran, attacked the U.S. Embassy in Beirut twice and destroyed the U.S. marine barracks at Beirut Airport, killing 241 people in all.

These acts completely refocused our attention on the potential threat posed by fundamentalist suicide terrorists through their capacity to penetrate our protective measures and cause high levels of death and destruction without warning. This is not to say that secular terrorists stopped their activities. The downing by Libyan agents of Pan-Am Flight 103 over Scotland in 1988 is just one example. But terrorists claiming fundamentalist religious motivation have generally taken center stage. The emergence of Hamas, the Palestinian Islamic Jihad, the Egyptian Islamic Group, and, most recently, Osama bin-Ladin's Al-Qa'idah organization, has attracted most of our attention over the past decade; and our resources have largely been devoted to terrorist threats from religious extremism.

The 1990's were marked by a long series of suicide bombings and assassinations by Hamas and the PIJ, bodily attacks on tourists by Egyptian militant groups, and the 1998 bombings of the U.S. Embassies in Nairobi and Dar es Salaam by suicide terrorists trained and equipped by Osama bin-Ladin's organization.

Fundamentalist terrorist groups have demonstrated that they can easily recruit new members from disillusioned elements of society. In some cases, the prospect of martyrdom actually increases these groups' appeal among the youth, who feel disenfranchised and are looking for ways to make a name for themselves and achieve special treatment for their families. Hamas and Hizballah have created parallel public institutions such as clinics, public health services and social-welfare organizations. This outreach to the community gives these groups a veneer of legitimacy and new avenues for recruitment of people willing to sacrifice their lives.

Osama bin-Ladin and his organization represent perhaps the most alarming trend in suicide terrorism emanating from the Middle East and South Asia. Bin-Ladin has created the first truly transnational fundamentalist terrorist enterprise, drawing recruits from Muslims across Asia, Africa, Europe and the Middle East. Willingness to be martyred in action appears to be the hallmark of some of these terrorists. Bin-Ladin has cultivated an unholy alliance among Islamic fundamentalist groups from different regions. And his organization has also avowed its intention to attain weapons of mass-destruction. The prospect of a fundamentalist suicide bomber with one of these weapons is indeed terrifying.

For those of us involved in making decisions concerning our government's effort to combat terrorism, the rise and prominence of suicide terrorism over the past two decades has presented unique problems and challenges. I hope this conference will help address and answer some of the questions that governments face in devising strategies to confront this type of terrorist. For example, how do terrorist groups motivate religious individuals to seek martyrdom in pursuit of a cause? What is in a suicide terrorist's mind? How do Islamic clerics and Islamic society view these fundamentalist groups and the individuals who sacrifice their lives? What is it about the Islamic religion as opposed to some others that enables fundamentalist groups to use Islam to justify suicide terrorism? And what can governments do to counter the lure of suicide terrorism?

Orthodox Islamic Perceptions
of Jihad and Martyrdom

Prof. Abdul Hadi Palazzi

*Director, Cultural Institute of the Italian Islamic Community,
Rome, Italy*

I want to thank the International Policy Institute for Counter-Terrorism for the invitation to this international conference to address such a distinguished and highly qualified audience.

I want to start by drawing a sharp distinction between traditional Islamic approaches to jihad and martyrdom, and the distortion of those values by radical movements, which promote terrorism and claim to do so in the name of Islam.

This distinction is clearly just one example of a more fundamental dualism and it enables us to understand in greater detail differences between the orthodox-traditional Islam, the religion that was revealed through the prophet Mohammed, whose main sources are the Qur'an and the prophetic tradition called Sunna in Arabic, and the contemporary ideology that is commonly referred to as Islamic fundamentalism.

As a Muslim scholar, I must point out from the outset that I reject the definitions of Islamic fundamentalism common in the contemporary media. As a matter of fact, I personally never use the terms Islamic fundamentalism or Islamic radicalism, but rather what I call "pseudo-Islamic radicalism." And this is because, in my humble opinion, fundamentalism is not one of the legitimate keys to understanding the Islamic message, but an evident distortion of Islamic values, an attempt to transform Islam from a religious tradition to a political ideology. Some Muslims who are deeply involved in the study of fundamentalism, support this view. For example, my friend and colleague Professor Halid Duran of Temple University of Philadelphia, who marks the distinction between orthodox Islamic doctrine and its political counterpart by calling the former "Islamic" and the latter "Islamist." On this debate, Professor Duran writes:

> Whether Islamists like the term "fundamentalism" or not, their understanding of religion resembles that of fundamentalists in other religions. That is not to say that Islamists are more religious or more genuinely Islamic than other Muslims. A common misunderstanding in the west is that Islamists are the one hundred percent among Muslims and that they are and represent the people of tradition. But this is not at all the case. Islamists, on the contrary, have a problem with the people of tradition, especially with the mystics. Islamism is a late 20th century totalitarianism. It follows in the wake of fascist and communist (ideologies), picking up from those and seeking to reify their methods of domination. Islamists mold tradition so as to serve to their political ends, and this causes them to clash with traditionalist Muslims who try to resist this manipulation of religion for power politics. Islamism is not a reaction of people feeling a loss of religious meaning, but a reaction to a sense of loss in the political sphere. It is a thrust for power, an attempt to conquer the state, not to regain independence for religion, and, least of all, independence for individual fate.
>
> Like most totalitarian ideologies, Islamism is utopian. Islamists seek to dominate the most advanced technologies, and in that sense they are modernists. But they are a model for an ideal society that takes inspiration from an idealized 17th century Arabia and a historical view of religion and human development in general. It is an anachronistic mode of thinking, in conflict with modern concepts of democracy, pluralism, and human rights.

Here the quotation from Professor Duran ends. It highlights relevant differences between traditional or orthodox Islam and Islamism as a way of understanding the link between religion and politics.

Few Muslims would deny that political commitment is part of Islamic ethics. Indeed, most agree with the Islamists, who insist that there is a clearly defined Islamic system, different from all other political systems. Islamists, however, refuse to accept a secular state that puts a member of a non-Muslim minority on equal footing with a member of a Muslim majority, or accords a woman equality with a man. But, according to traditional Islamic theology, prophets are sent to dwell among human beings to teach them some necessary truths about the nature of God, about ethics and about actions and omissions which lead to prosperity in this world and beatitude in the world hereafter.

Sometimes the prophets preach in a world where social organization does not exist at all and need to establish political forms, and this, according to the Islamist belief, explains the case of Moses as a leader of the children of Israel in the exodus from Egypt, or the position of Mohammed as a governor of a state centered in Medina. But Islamic orthodoxy teaches that this happens by accident, and that political leadership is not among the necessary elements of the prophet's mastery. As a matter of fact, the Qur'an uses different titles to describe the prophet Mohammed, but none of these refers to a political function. The Qur'an says that Mohammed has been sent as an "admonisher," as a "warner," as "someone who calls to God," as "a shining light." But it never says that that he was sent as a political leader or as a head of state.

Islamists, on the other hand, take the opposite view. They maintain that the diffusion of Islam cannot be separated from the creation of what they call "the Islamic State." The role of Muslim scholar is immediately confused with the role of leader of a political movement or party.

Islamists incessantly repeat that Islam is both religion and government, and this can be seen as the slogan for their creed. But they fail to prove that the word, Islam, does indeed refer to both religion and government. In Arabic, references to Islam in this sense are not found in the Qur'an or in the sayings of the prophet Mohammed, and are not quoted in any of the ancient authoritative Islamic sources. As a matter of fact, the slogan joining religion and politics was coined by Taqiyyu-d-din Ibn Taymiyyah, a scholar who lived during the 13th and 14th centuries of the Christian era— and he was condemned to life imprisonment for his numerous heresies.

Those who repeat the slogan, "Islam is religion and government," are the same people who, for instance, ceaselessly advocate the liberation of Jerusalem from the hands of the Jews. But unfortunately for them, Ibn Taymiyyah, from whom they take their slogan, strongly denies any special role for Jerusalem in Islam. Ibn Taymiyyah openly writes, "there is no Muslim holy place in Jerusalem." But his followers claim to be fighting for the liberation of Jerusalem in his name. This a clear example of how confused an ideology Islamism is, and of how contradictions are simply passed over in silence.

While many western researchers tend to describe Islamism as a form of "resurgent" Islam, traditional Muslim scholars read its appearance as a symptom of secularization, a reshaping of their religion in the form of a modern ideological totalitarianism. This is especially evident in the Islamist deformation of the role of jihad. In the original meaning of the term, jihad is not limited to military action, but generally means "striving hard towards a certain goal." According to sayings of the prophet Mohammed in the compilation known as *Sahih Al-BU.K.hari*, "Delivery is the jihad for a woman," while, for someone whose parents are old, jihad is taking care of them. On the contrary, the military aspect of jihad is not a case of spreading the religion under false pretenses, but is a form of defense against religious persecution. This is the original Qur'anic notion of jihad, and, for instance, we read in the Qur'an, "To those against whom war is made, permission is given [to defend themselves], because they have been wronged, and verily, God is most powerful for their aid. [They are] those who have been expelled from their homes [for no cause] except that they say, 'our lord is God.' Did not God check one people by means of another, there would surely have been pulled down monasteries, churches, synagogues, and mosques, in which the name of God is commemorated in abandoned measure." (22, 39-40)

It is clear, then, that military jihad is not meant to serve as a key to expand a given situation, but rather as a way to defend the rights of those who are persecuted because of their religion. The verses I have quoted clearly state the deprivation of religious freedom as justification for defense. And this statement refers not only to mosques, but also to monasteries, churches, and synagogues, places where God's name is frequently worshipped. These are all among the sites that must be protected.

Apart from these stipulations, the legitimate form of military jihad in ancient Islamic sources is based on various rules and conditions. Condition number one is that jihad must be waged by a regular army battling against another army. Terrorist acts against a civilian population are simply not included in the definition of jihad. The collection of prophetic sayings mentioned above states that when the prophet Mohammed learned that a certain group of jihad fighters had killed several women, he raised his hands to heaven and prayed, "Oh God, be my witness that my hands are innocent of this crime."

The second stipulation is that even when self-defense is justified, the reaction must not be extreme. A typical example of this is presented in the historical story of Moses and the Egyptians as narrated in the Qur'an. To defend an Israelite, who was being beaten by an Egyptian, Moses killed the Egyptian himself. There is no doubt that the Israelite was a member of an oppressed people, someone who was persecuted because of his religion and faith, while the Egyptian was the oppressor. According to the basic rule, this event might well have even been described as a legitimate form of jihad, but the Qur'an does not support this opinion and condemns Moses' reaction as extreme. In the Qur'an we find that Moses himself asked for forgiveness for his actions. The Qur'an recounts the story as follows: "And when Moses entered the city its inhabitants were in a state of feeble-mindedness, and he found therein two men fighting, one of his religion and the other of his enemies. And the one who was of his religion sought his help against the one who was of his enemies. So Moses struck the latter with his fist, and thereby caused his death. Then Moses said, 'This is Satan's doing and he is indeed an enemy and a powerful leader of evil.' He then cried, 'Oh my lord, I have wronged my soul, will thou forgive me?' And He forgave him, for He is most forgiving and merciful." (28, 15-16) Along the same lines, another Qur'anic verse states, "And fight in the way of God against those who fight against you, but do not exaggerate. Verily, God does not love those who exagerate." (2, 190)

The third condition, a condition that is currently quite blatantly ignored, is that when the former enemy is ready to cease hostilities and seeks an opportunity to achieve peace, it is the duty of Muslims to stop fighting and accept a peaceful solution. The Qur'an says: "Make ready for those who fight you with whatever you can muster of armed forces and mount blockades at the frontier, whereby you might deter the enemy and also those enemies that you don't know, but God knows them well. But if they are inclined toward peace, incline thee toward peace too and put thy trust in God." (8, 60-61)

Moreover, martyrdom in Islam is the worthy condition of one that forfeits his life to bear witness to the truth. The Arabic word *shahid,* often translated into English as martyr, etymologically means "witness," someone whose existence is a living testimony, even after his death. The Qur'an states: "Think not of those who are slain in the cause of God as dead. Nay, they are alive in the presence of the Lord and are granted gifts from him."(3, 169)

But concerning suicide, this act is manifestly forbidden by the most authoritative sources of Islamic law. These laws clearly forbid suicide even when the individual committing suicide is supposedly doing so for a good cause. The Qur'an clearly admonishes, "And do not kill yourself, for God is indeed merciful to you." Qur'anic interpreters explain that the verse and the lines on committing suicide represent a direct negation of divine mercy. In another verse the Qur'an states, "And do not throw yourself into destruction with your own hands." Interpreters explain that "throwing yourself into destruction with your own hands" refers to committing suicide. Even the status of suicides during the year after they commit the act is described in a saying of the prophet Mohammed contained in Muslim and other authoritative compilations. This tradition states, "Whoever kills himself with a knife will be in hell forever, stabbing himself in the stomach; Whoever kills himself by drinking poison will eternally drink poison in the hell fire; And whoever kills himself by falling off a mountain will forever fall in the fire of hell."

In the light of all this conclusive evidence, one must inevitably ask an obvious question: How is it possible for certain groups, who claim to be Islamic and even to represent Islam, to advocate both terrorism against civil population and suicide terrorism? It is my opinion that this is just one of the fruits of a foul theory based on the distortion and falsification not only of these, but also of many other basic tenets of Islamic belief. Although the above-mentioned reasons provide ample explanation for the extreme consequences, the roots must be traced to the beginnings of the Wahhabi movement in Arabia. In my opinion, grasping the nature and theoretical apparatus of the Wahhabis is essential to the comprehension of contemporary Islamist radicalism and also to the conception of possible counter-measures. Moreover, in traditional Islam it is clear that military jihad and all other forms of physical jihad only constitute the external aspect of jihad, while the inner dimension of jihad is the struggle that every Muslim undertakes to purify his soul against his defects and egotism.

According to a well-known tradition, after coming back from a military expedition, the prophet Mohammed said, "We are returning from the lesser jihad and we are moving toward the greater jihad." He was then asked, "What do you mean by the greater jihad?" and he replied, "It is the jihad against one's soul, the jihad against our own limitations, our own defects." This is a statement that has always been quoted by Islamic scholars as a way to explain the inner dimension of jihad. Denial of this tradition was one of the theoretical bases of the Wahhabis.

The Wahhabis made every effort to quote all possible arguments to prove that this tradition is not authentic. According to their theory, the greater jihad simply does not exist. They define the jihad as a purely military struggle. But this evasion regarding the meaning of jihad can contribute considerably to a true comprehension of the present situation, where the jihad is misconstrued to imply terrorism. Crimes against a civilian population can, on the basis of the sources we have quoted, be considered a form of legitimate jihad for the simple reason that they are based upon a most basic human passion. Since fighting human passions is in itself a greater jihad, then rebutting those who abuse Islamic belief to legitimatize terrorism is also a very important expression of the true jihad.

As to the origins of the Wahhabi movement, we must keep in mind that the beginning of the 18th century of the common era witnessed the emergence of a movement in the Arabian peninsula that shattered the spiritual equilibrium of the Islamic world. The result was an explosive profusion of primitive violence and anti-intellectual tendencies. This early call for a return to the origins was in fact the primary scream of primitivism that destroyed the basic variety of the Islamic culture. It eradicated the proliferation of opinions, the plurality of schools, and this was replaced by a monolithic, simple-minded dogmatism. It is important to comprehend that the movement started with missionary activity among desert Bedouins. Mohammed Ibn Abd al-Wahab, the founder of the Wahhabi movement, began preaching his doctrine in the desert of Najd. There he met Muhammad Ibn Sa'ud, the leader of a gang of roving raiders, whose profession was robbing pilgrims and travelers in the desert of Najd. Like most of the Bedouins living in that area, they were completely illiterate. And Ibn Abd al-Wahab had no difficulty in convincing them of his ideas. Ibn Sa'ud and Ibn Abd al-Wahab made a deal whereby the former was proclaimed political leader, Emir, and the latter was proclaimed the religious authority, the Sheik. And what is impressive is that for the first time in the history of Islam, a Sheik issued a religious decree, a *fatwa*, whereby all non-Wahhabi Muslims were openly declared apostates and idol worshippers. This new doctrine stated that only a very limited, strict group comprises the true Muslims, while all the rest of the Muslims are, to use their terminology, the people of apostasy. This gave Ibn Sa'ud the cloak of religious legitimacy he needed to persecute innocent people. His gang was no longer a mob of traveling thugs and his victims were no longer innocent people. Now Ibn Sa'ud's goons were "fighters for jihad," authorized to murder "unbelievers." For the first time in history, jihad was proclaimed against Muslims, and even against the Ottoman Empire whose Sultan was considered the heir of the prophet Muhammad and the highest Islamic authority.

To understand the consequences of this situation we can quote from an important source, the *Fitnah al-Wahhabiyya* (the Wahhabi Sedition), written by Ahmad Zayni ad-Dahlan al Makki ash-Shaf'i, the chief Mufti of Mecca during the time that Wahhabism was rapidly spreading. He wrote:

> In 1802, Christian era, the Wahhabis marched with large armies to the area of at-Tayf. In Dhu al-Qa'dah of the same year they laid siege to the area occupied by Muslims, defeated them, and murdered all the people, including men, women, and children. They also lauded the Muslims longing for possessions, and only a few people escaped their barbarism. They even stole gifts from the grave of the prophet Mohammed, took all the gold that was there, and engaged in many similar acts of sacrilege. After that they laid siege to Mecca and surrounded it from all directions to tighten the siege. They blocked the roads to the city and prevented supplies from reaching it. This caused great hardship to the people of Mecca, for supplies became unaffordable and completely unavailable. The situation was such that for some months people resorted to eating dogs.

These events, as briefly summarized above, rent the face of the Islamic world. Consider that Mecca and Medina, the two centers from which Islam spread to the rest of the world, were no longer the nucleus for the dissemination of traditional heritage. They had become places where traditional aspects of worship, according to the established schools of Islamic students, were suppressed and replaced by a primitive and illiterate cult that was propagated through violence and aggression. But the drama did not stop there. Like all other forms of totalitarian ideology, the very nature of Wahhabism dictated the need for expansion. Its aspirations were firstly to conquer the whole Islamic world and then to spread its influence beyond those boundaries. The establishment of a world center in Mecca for Wahhabi propaganda, the organization called 'World Islamic League', was the final step of a plan whose goal was to replace Orthodox Islam with the puritanical so-called *Salafi* school, the name by which Wahhabis identify themselves. By doing so, dogmatic uniformity began to stifle the humane and enlightened Islamic tradition, and the distortion of a national jihad and martyrdom played a central role in the expansion of their ideology.

The main instrument for the Wahhabization of the Arab society was the organization called 'The Muslim Brotherhood.' This organization became a sort of international network, as it is to this very day, and it is able to spread its tentacles in most Arab countries because of its grass-roots influence. To give a clear example, when a radical militant member of this organization is poor, ignorant or fanatic, his life dream can only be to throw stones, to commit acts of terrorism, or to kill as many innocent people as a suicide bomber can. But for a militant who is cleverer, his life aspiration is not to be involved in this kind of violent activity. His dream is to travel abroad as a student, to become a full-time professional propagandist. By doing so, he will spend his life visiting mosques and expanding the network in the United States, England, France, Germany or Italy, living in any of those places as a propagator. And because their doctrine is that people involved in social work may keep the money they collect, they are able to pocket funds not only from their central organization, but from local members too.

What then is the possible solution? I must say that most of the progressive Arab countries are aware of the difficulties connected to the expansion of this network, and they have ways to restrict and limit the activities of the fundamentalists. Unfortunately, the real risk is that those same groups that are deemed illegal in many Arab countries may become the official representatives of Muslim immigrants in Western governments. This could well happen in the future. And this, I believe, is one of the dangers that we must stress: namely, that there exists a close connection between the fundamentalist network in countries of origin and the same network in the country of immigration.

I want to conclude by noting that my friend, Dr. Asher Eder, the Jewish Co-Chairman of the Islam-Israel Fellowship, has written an illuminating paper called "Peace is Possible between Ishmael and Israel according to the Qur'an." I truly believe that this paper is of supreme importance and I was honored when asked to write its preface. This paper can help non-Muslims to understand that the teachings of the Qur'an are radically different than the claims made by the fundamentalists. It can also show Muslims that the hatred targeted at Israel and Jews, which features so prominently in their propaganda, is by no means supported by their religion.

With the passing of time, the influence of the Islam-Israel Fellowship has grown steadily. I take pleasure in noting the fact that the President of Uzbekistan, Islam Karimov, recently founded a new international Islamic University in Tashkent. Among this university's main goals is the training of moderate Imams and Muslim religious leaders instructed in refuting fundamentalism and in promoting dialogue between Jews, Christians, and Muslims.

This fact is highly significant because it could mean that for the first time an anti-fundamentalist network has the chance to take root. Admittedly, when compared to the huge worldwide influence of the fundamentalist network, its role is reminiscent of the struggle between David and Goliath. Nevertheless, there is good reason to be hopeful. And this is indeed my hope, that the creation of this anti-fundamentalist, moderate Muslim network will act as an important force in countering the expansion of the fundamentalist network. As the Qur'an says, "How oft, by God's will, hath a small force vanquished a big one? Verily, God is with those who steadfastly persevere." (2, 249)

Suicide Terrorism:
Development and main characteristics

Yoram Schweitzer

Director, ICT Educational Project

Over the past two decades suicide terrorism has become an ever-spreading phenomenon. Fifteen different terrorist organizations in twelve different countries resorted to the use of suicide tactics against their enemies. As of February 2000, about 275 suicide incidents have occurred (see Table 1).

When suicide terrorism was first introduced in the Middle East, it seemed that this new phenomenon was invincible and that it might change the innate imbalance between terror groups and their rival governments. This did not in fact occur.

Looking at the history of terrorism, it can be seen that suicide attacks are in actuality a very old *modus operandi*. In ancient times two notorious sects, the Jewish Sicairis and the Islamic Hashishiyun, became infamous for such attacks. In the 18th century, suicide tactics were used on the Malabar Coast of Southwestern India, in Atjeh in Northern Sumatra, and in Mindanao and Sulu in the Southern Philippines. In all of these places Muslims carried out suicide attacks in their fight against Western hegemony and colonial rule.[1]

However, contemporary suicide terrorism differs from such historical tactics, just as the whole phenomenon of terrorism differs from ancient modes of warfare.

Modern suicide terrorism is aimed at causing devastating physical damage, through which it inflicts profound fear and anxiety. Its goal is to produce a negative psychological effect on an entire population, rather than just the victims of the actual attack.

---

[1] "Religious Suicide in Islamic Asia," Stephen Fredric Dale, Department of History, Ohio State University.

The relatively high number of casualties guaranteed in such attacks, which are usually carried out in crowded areas, ensures full media coverage. Thus, suicide terrorism ranks with other spectacular methods such as blowing up airplanes in midair or using Weapons of Mass Destruction as a sure means to win maximum effect.

For the purposes of this paper a suicide terror attack is defined as *a politically motivated violent attack perpetrated by a self-aware individual (or individuals) who actively and purposely causes his own death through blowing himself up along with his chosen target. The perpetrator's ensured death is a precondition for the success of his mission.* (See also Boaz Ganor's definition.)

Thus this paper deals with a very specific kind of attack. It does not deal with very high-risk terror operations that leave only a small chance of survival to their perpetrators. Such attacks as the Japanese Red Army's (JRA) attack at Lod airport in 1972, Abu Nidal's attack on a synagogue in Istanbul in 1986 and the PFLP-GC hand-glider attack on an army barracks in Kiryat Shmona in 1987 fall outside the scope of this paper. Also excluded were the self-inflicted deaths of members of terrorist organizations, such as the famous leaders of the German Bader-Meinhof gang (1977) or the fatal self-starvation of Bobby Sands of the P.I.RA (1981).

This paper gives a general overview of the modern history of suicide terrorism worldwide, focusing on its main characteristics and the various aims and motivations of the terror groups involved.

The current phenomenon of suicide terrorism has usually involved terrorists carrying explosive charges concealed on their bodies or carried by various vehicles, usually cars, trucks, or boats. In some instances the explosives were transported by bicycle, or loaded on a pack animal (see Table 3).

Hizballah suicide terrorism

Suicide terror attacks started in Lebanon in April 1983. A small— and until then unknown—group by the name of Hizballah directed a number of suicide attacks against Western targets. The first attack was directed at the American embassy in Beirut (April 1983), followed by attacks on the U.S. Marines headquarters and the French Multinational Force (October 1983). The last two were executed simultaneously and resulted in 300 casualties and dozens of wounded. The latter attack made an indelible impression on world public opinion and terror organizations alike.

After the withdrawal of the Western forces from Lebanon, Hizballah redirected its suicide activities in Lebanon against Israeli Defense Forces (convoys, posts and border passages) and against South Lebanese Army posts. Hizballah henceforth significantly decreased its use of this *modus operandi* to one attack per year or less. Despite this, it enjoyed its legacy as the pioneer of suicide bombings in the region.

The aims of Hizballah suicide missions changed and developed over the course of time. Initially, Hizballah was interested in building up it image as a power. Since it had been until then a small group, little-known even in Lebanon, let alone in the rest of the world, the introduction of this new and devastating *modus operandi* served the goal of gaining local and global publicity and notoriety.

Hizballah also presented its Iranian patrons with a valuable image for the spread of the Islamic revolution. The readiness of Shi'ite terrorists, utterly fearless and ready to sacrifice themselves for the defense of the "oppressed of the earth" was an important propaganda instrument for both Iran and Hizballah.

Hizballah's suicide attacks were successful in driving the foreign UN Peacekeeping forces out of Lebanon. The attacks also caused the Israeli army to withdraw from the heartland of central Lebanon to a narrow strip in the South.

Suicide attacks also served the organization as a weapon of retaliation and deterrence against Israel. After the Israeli Airforce killed Hizballah's secretary general, Abas Musawi, in February 1992, the organization carried out a suicide attack against the Israeli embassy in Buenos Aires (March 1992), killing 29 people and wounding 250.

In 1994 Hizballah executed another such attack in the same city, against the "AMIA" building of the local Jewish community, in retaliation for an I.D.F. aerial attack in Lebanon against a Hizballah training camp in Ein Dardara.

Lebanon saw around 50 suicide attacks between 83-99. The Shiite organizations, Hizballah and Amal, were responsible for about half of these. The other half is attributed to five other groups espousing a non-religious nationalist ideology. Impressed by the effectiveness of Hizballah's attacks in precipitating the withdrawal of the "foreigners" from Lebanon, these nationalist groups followed suit.

Hizballah also influenced a number of terrorist organizations in other countries. Occasionally this influence went beyond merely being a role model.

In Kuwait two suicide attacks were attributed to El-Dawa, a local Kuwaiti-Shiite fundamentalist group. The first was carried out in December 1983 as one in a series of otherwise "conventional" attacks on American, French and Kuwaiti interests. The second attack was directed at the Emir al-Sabah, in May 1985. Hizballah's direct involvement was proven when the Kuwaiti authorities arrested and tried seventeen people, among them Mustafa Bader-el-Din, a prominent terrorist in Hizballah's external terror apparatus. Hizballah's continuous and extensive efforts to release him and his partners came to be known as the "Dawa Seventeen" affair.

The LTTE

One of the groups that followed Hizballah—even exceeding it in both execution and number of incidents—was the LTTE, the Tamil separatist group in Sri Lanka.

The LTTE is unequivocally the most effective and brutal terrorist organization ever to utilize suicide terrorism. Between July 1987 and February 2000 it has carried out ·168 suicide terror attacks in Sri Lanka and India, leaving thousands of innocent bystanders dead or wounded.[2] Its suicide unit, the "Black Panthers," is

---

[2] Rohan Gunaratna, Lecture at ICT Conference: Countering Suicide Terrorism, February 2000.

comprised of both men and women. One characteristic unique to the LTTE is that every member of the group carries a cyanide capsule around his/her neck, which he or she may consume upon capture in order not to disclose the group's secrets. The members of the "Black Panthers" unit have demonstrated their continuous readiness to die when they were surrounded by security forces. In many instances they blew themselves up or bit cyanide capsules rather than risk captivity and subsequent interrogation which could force them to betray their comrades.

The LTTE has directed its attacks primarily against the highest Sri-Lankan and Indian political and military personnel. It is the only organization that succeeded in assassinating two heads of state. Former Indian Prime Minister Rajiv Gandhi was assassinated in May 1991 by a female suicide-bomber while campaigning for re-election. Sri Lanka president Prendesa was assassinated in 1993 by a male suicide-bomber who had infiltrated the president's inner circle, and even lived at the president's premises for about one year before executing his mission.

The LTTE persists in its efforts to eliminate the ruling elite in Sri Lanka. In December 1999 it tried to assassinate the current president, Mrs. Kumaratunga, who survived the attack but lost an eye. On 5 January 2000, the Prime Minister's residence was attacked by a suicide-bomber, apparently in an attempt to assassinate the Defence Minister. Neither the Prime Minister nor the Defense Minister was injured. The LTTE also killed several senior army commanders, as well as prominent Tamil politicians who cooperated with the government in order to find a peaceful solution in Sri Lanka.

Due to the LTTE's intensive suicide campaign, Sri-Lankan politicians seem reluctant openly to confront or declare an all-out war against the group.

Suicide Terrorism in Israel

In Israel, suicide terrorism started in 1993. The Hamas (*Harkat el-MU.K.awma el Islamiya* or "The Islamic Resistance Movement") and the Palestinian Islamic Jihad (PIJ) carried out about 30 suicide terror attacks which caused about 120 fatalities and wounded hundreds.

Hamas and the PIJ were also inspired and assisted by Hizballah. The PIJ leadership maintained close relationships with Iran and Hizballah from the early 80's. The relationship between Hamas and Hizballah gained momentum after Israel deported a few hundred Hamas operatives to Lebanon in 1992. There they established a close liaison with Hizballah and the Iranian Revolutionary Guards. Both groups learned suicide-terrorism techniques in Lebanon.

Hamas and the PIJ focused their initial suicide attacks on military targets in the "Territories," but quite rapidly shifted their attacks to civilians in Israel's central cities and crowded areas. The two Palestinian Sunni fundamentalist groups succeeded in inflicting a high number of casualties among the Israeli civilian population; this had a profound negative impact on the Israeli public's sense of personal security. This effect was intensified by the fact that the terror campaign accompanied a peace process, which was supposed to bring tranquility to the relationship between Israelis and Palestinians. Another influential factor was the continuity of the attacks; sometimes they were a weekly occurrence. The suicide factor in the Palestinian terror campaign thus had a strategic impact on the Israel-Palestinian peace-process.

At the beginning of March 2000, Hamas attempted to carry out 3 to 5 suicide attacks in Israeli cities. The operation was thwarted when Israeli security forces liquidated the cell before it could act. Two of the cell's leaders escaped and were later caught in Nablus by the Palestinian security forces as part of a joint Israeli-Palestinian operation.

Egyptian Terrorism

The Egyptian terror groups also contributed their share to the suicide phenomenon. Each of the two leading groups, the Gama'a al-Islamiya and the Egyptian Islamic Jihad (Jihad Group) carried out one attack. The Gama'a al-Islamiya operated in Croatia in October 1995, attacking a local police station in Rijake. This was in retaliation for the disappearance of one of the group's leaders in

Croatia and his eventual extradition to Egypt. The Jihad Group used two suicide bombers to destroy the Egyptian embassy in Pakistan in November 1995, causing 15 fatalities and wounding dozens. This attack was in retaliation for Pakistani-Egyptian cooperation in extraditing terrorists to Egypt.

It should be noticed that both groups avoided using such tactics on Egyptian soil. This can be attributed to their reluctance to alienate their constituency in Egypt by causing the indiscriminate death of innocent bystanders. The greater efficiency of the security forces in Egypt as compared to that in other countries may also have played a role.

The PKK

Another group that has used suicide terror attacks in the past is the Kurdistan Worker's Party (PKK).

The PKK has carried out a total of 21 suicide attacks or attempted attacks (15 attacks were actually carried out and 6 were intercepted). Its suicide campaign started on 30 June 1996 and ceased on 5 July 1999, at the decision of its leader, Abdullah Ocalan. This terror campaign caused relatively low casualties: 19 were killed and 138 were wounded.[3]

The PKK resorted to suicide terrorism at a time when it was facing heavy military setbacks in Southeast Turkey, which had had an adverse effect on the morale of its members. Since the group's terrorist activities had declined constantly between 1994-1996, the organization was seeking an effective means to reverse this trend and to boost the morale of its fighters. Suicide missions were therefore chosen as a consolidating tool. They served as a demonstration of the PKK's capability to operate and to damage their enemies. The attacks demonstrated the perpetrator's supreme willingness to sacrifice everything for the Kurdish national goals. For some time, such attacks were used for retaliatory purposes.

---

[3] Professor Dogu Ergil, Lecture at ICT Conference: Countering Suicide Terrorism, February 2000.

Al-Qaidah

Al-Qaidah, headed by Osama bin-Ladin, is the last group to have resorted to suicide attacks, and has a close operational connection to the Egyptian groups. Al-Qaidah was responsible for two of the most spectacular and lethal suicide attacks in recent times. The simultaneous attacks against the American embassies in Nairobi and in Dar-e-Salaam in August 1998 resulted in 300 fatalities and five thousand wounded, most of them innocent local bystanders. (tables 2 and 3.)

Women's role in suicide terrorism

Women have played an important role in the terrorist activity of some of the prominent groups that use suicide terrorism. In general this prominence is limited to the organizations with a nationalist orientation. The fundamentalist Islamic terror groups have never let women to take part in their terrorist activities, let alone in suicide terrorism.

The nationalist groups, such as the PKK, the LTTE, and the P.P.S., enable women to participate in their most extreme attacks. The leaders of these groups often exploit female members' profound desire to prove equality with their male peers and encourage—sometimes even manipulate them—to "volunteer" for such missions.

Women account for a high percentage of suicide attacks: In the LTTE they participated in about 30% to 40% of the group's overall suicide activities. In the PKK, women carried out 11 out of 15 successful attacks, while the perpetrators of 3 of the 6 attacks that were intercepted were women; in all, a total of 14 out of 21 suicide attackers, 66 % of the total were women. In the P.P.S./S.S.N.P. (Syrian Socialist Nationalist Party), women took part in 5 out of the group's 12 suicide activities.

The reasons for using women in particular in this kind of operation evolved from a variety of considerations on the part of the organizations. However, all of these groups deceptively used the innocent appearance of a "pregnant" woman in order to bypass heavy security arrangements while approaching their targets. All of them take advantage of women's desire to prove their abilities and devotion to the organization and to their supreme leader. In several cases, especially in P.P.S., there were romantic feelings involved.

Concluding remarks

Looking at suicide terrorism from a perspective of seventeen years, one may conclude that it has not been a "winning card" in the hands of terror organizations; nor has it changed dramatically the inherent imbalance between states and terror organizations in favor of the terrorists. Nonetheless, it has proven to be an effective instrument in the service of the terrorist's agenda.

In certain situations involving the presence of military forces on foreign soil or during a delicate period of political negotiations during a peace process, suicide attacks may have a profound negative influence. For example, Hizballah was successful in its campaign to expel the M.N.F. from Lebanon. Hamas was successful in delaying the implementation of the Oslo accords in the Middle East, and the LTTE succeeded in halting the deployment of Indian peace keeping troops to Sri Lanka and brought about the subsequent postponement of peace talks in Sri Lanka.

However, most of the groups that were involved in suicide terrorism either stopped using it or eventually reduced it significantly. Thus, suicide terrorism is not increasing, though it may spread in future to other areas of conflict, given the "copy-cat" nature of terrorism.

The greatest potential risk suicide terrorism may pose in future is if terrorists carry out operations combined with other spectacular tactics such as blowing up airplanes or the use of Weapons of Mass Destruction. Such a combination will increase immensely the death toll of a single terror attack and will have a shocking psychological effect on public morale. At this level suicide terrorism would constitute a genuine strategic threat, and would probably be confronted as such.

TABLE 1

Number of Attacks by Organization

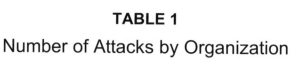

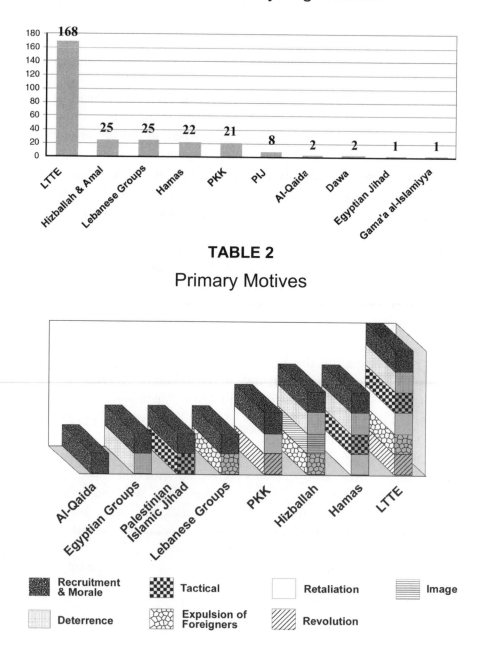

TABLE 2

Primary Motives

TABLE 3

Attacks by Modus Operandi

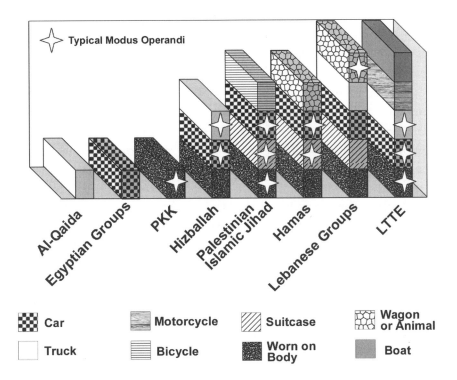

The Islamic Legitimacy
of Suicide Terrorism

Reuven Paz

Academic Director, ICT

The difference in perception between the West and Islam is evident in the very terminology used to describe suicide terrorism. While Western political culture uses the term "suicide terrorism," Islamists refer to the phenomenon as "Istishad"—martyrdom and self-sacrifice in the name of Allah.

When researching not only suicide terrorism but the Islamist phenomenon in general, we must bear in mind one very important fact. We must take into account that perhaps the greatest success of Islamist movements in the past 20 or 30 years is their ability to present their doctrines to the general public—not only in the Arab world but elsewhere as well—as true Islam. Indeed, their doctrine has become as popular as, if not more popular than, the actual religion.

The moderates mentioned by Professor Palazzi—those who reputedly represent the origins of Orthodox Islam and perhaps even what we would call "true Islam'—are in some places a distinct minority. The Wahhabi Movement, the Muslim Brotherhood, and the Islamic Jihad have all succeeded in convincing not only their own members and sympathizers, but a large section of the wider Muslim community, that they are to be regarded as the sole representatives of true Islam. It is noteworthy that so many have become convinced that the teachings and statements of such groups represent the true religion.

With regard to suicide as it is regarded in Islam, when I began to research the rationalization of suicide, not only by the Hamas, but by Hizballah, the Palestinian Islamic Jihad, and other movements, I found that the subject is mostly ignored by Muslim scholars or researchers. The same is true of Western academics dealing with Islamist history or Islam in general. The only article about suicide in Islam published in the West dates back to 1946. It was written by the late Frantz Rosental, and since then no academic scholar in the West has dealt with the subject. This is no coincidence, as the issue has also been ignored by Muslim society itself. This is something that should be taken into consideration when analyzing the issue from the security standpoint.

The foundations of suicide terrorism in the Arab world

A very interesting analysis of the phenomenon of suicide terrorism was written by the Egyptian sociologist Dr. Hudash El-Sharawi, of the Kazic University in Egypt. This is one of the institutions of higher learning in Egypt that serve as hothouses for intensive Islamist activity. It was here that the Palestinian Islamic Jihad Movement was founded by Shiqaqi, Shalach, Abdel-Aziz Ode, and others.

El-Sharawi's analysis was written following the June '95 attempt on the life of Egyptian President Mubarak in Ethiopia. He pointed out that we are dealing with youngsters who are at the age of fruitful creativity, but at the same time are under a lot of pressure, which impels them to act. It is thus easy to exploit them, and to recruit them as soldiers into a group that serves as a substitute for traditional units such as the family or tribe.

To the group member who is sent to kill and to be killed, death is presented as martyrdom—an act that will bring him closer to Allah. The individual who puts such ideas into a youngster's mind turns him into a ticking time-bomb, having first molded his personality in accordance with the needs of the new social group and its interests. The group programs him so that he will explode at any given time as if by a remote control detonator. In educating its members, the group uses totally different means than those employed by the former social framework. For while society plants its values slowly and gradually throughout childhood and youth, with the aim of establishing continuity, the new alternate group advocates swift indoctrination and exploits the most sacred means to appeal to the soul, such as religious belief. The group imbues its orders and prohibitions with a sense of religious holiness, so that its rulings cannot be disputed. In this way it inculcates an extreme level of self-discipline and prevents independent thinking.

In the 1980's a Lebanese sociologist by the name of Waji Kosrani wrote the following about the Shiites' struggle in Lebanon:

> Religion plays an important role in the resistance, and the Islamist culture has created a psychological atmosphere of willingness to fight and sacrifice to the death. Among Lebanese youngsters we can trace a permanent willingness to die for the sake of the greater social group. This is the consequence of the fact that the perception of the group in Southern Lebanon is rooted in the Islamist religion and the behavior of the group, which is based upon partnership and cooperation.

This combination of religious and social elements in Islamist societies is the key to understanding the phenomenon of what we term "suicide terrorism," or what Islamist movements call "self-sacrifice" or "Istishad." What we actually have here is a combination of religious justification and religious interpretation, together with social factors rooted in the surrounding society. This society sees itself as oppressed by what it views as a much stronger force. But on the other hand, it is also a society striving to shape its future and its future state, as in the case of the Palestinians. It is struggling not only against these powerful external enemies, but also against what it views as internal enemies—the secular or nationalist forces within society.

Islamist suicide terrorism in the Middle East

We do not observe this phenomenon of suicide terrorism as part of the internal struggle of Islamist groups within the Arab world, or inside the various Arab countries—neither in Algeria, Egypt, Jordan, nor in any other Arab country where terrorism is carried out by Islamist groups. There are definite reasons for this—why the two places where such crimes of terrorism have been carried are Lebanon and the Palestinian arena—including Israel itself and the territories of what is now termed "the Palestinian Authority."

What we are witnessing here is not only Islamist groups fighting for religious principles, but also the basic foundations of two social movements struggling to shape their future. In Lebanon, there is the struggle within the Shiite community against the Amal movement, which they regard as the most secular group of Shiites. Secondly, this community is struggling against the other sects in Lebanon, whom they regard as infidels. Thirdly—and it would be wise to bear this in mind despite the fact that you will often hear how ardently Syria supports Hizballah terrorism—in the long run the Shiites will also have to fight the messages of the Syrian regime as well as the Syrian dominance over Lebanon.

In the Palestinian case, with regard both to Hamas to the Palestinian Islamic Jihad, we also observe several of the same factors at work. Here, too, the struggle is twofold. One struggle is, of course, against the external enemy, the Israelis. I shall subsequently elaborate upon the struggle against the Jews in general because the latter plays an essential role in the rationalization of suicide terrorism. However, the Islamist movements are also struggling—for the moment only on the political level, for obvious reasons—against the Palestinian Authority, or, in other words, the Palestinian National Movement. The latter was represented in the past by the PLO, and is now by the Palestinian Authority. The struggle is over the shape of the future Palestinian independent state if and when it is established.

I wish to emphasize that here we are dealing not only with a phenomenon rooted in religious principles, but also with a phenomenon that seeks to convey a social message, mainly in Palestine and Lebanon, by means of social movements.

The religious justification of suicide terrorism

I will address first the religious elements justifying self-sacrifice or suicide terrorism. There are disputes in these matters between Islamic scholars and Islamist movements. To those observing the phenomenon of Islamist terrorist activity from the outside it may appear that such activity is easy to implement and easy to decide. However, this is not the case. The matter is controversial, and very few Islamic scholars have given the Islamist movements a religious ruling, or "Fatwa," to carry out their operations.

I would even go a step further. In the case of the Lebanese Hizballah, even Sherf Muhammad Senfadlala himself, the spiritual father, or, let's say, the religious authority of Hizballah in Lebanon, publicly expressed his reservations throughout the 1980's against repeated use of these methods. He warned against exaggeration among youth in using these methods of suicide terrorism, for two reasons. For one thing, he, along with many others, wished to prevent this phenomenon from becoming too widespread. The massive use of suicide terrorism could violate one of the most important prohibitions of Islam—that of killing oneself or committing suicide. The second reason may appear to be contradictory to the perceptions of outside observers, particularly politicians and the media. This is that there is a good deal of logic behind the activities of Islamist organizations in general, and particularly the Hamas and Hizballah. In the case of Hamas, its behavior is based not only on the logic of pragmatism, but also on the organizational doctrines of the Muslim Brotherhood with which the Hamas is typically affiliated.

Suicide terrorism and Israel

However, there is one factor that can be said to supercede all other elements. The perception of the struggle between Islam and Judaism is actually the main justification for the general use of terrorism, and particularly for suicide bombing. Consider that the two main venues where Islamist suicide terrorism occurs are connected, whether directly or indirectly, with Israel. The United States also plays a background role, and at least in one case, the French were victims—in Beirut in 1983. But the operations are carried out mainly against Israel. I shall not go into great detail, but in brief I must point out the common ground shared by most of the Arab Islamist groups.

Please note that I prefer not to use the term "fundamentalist groups," but instead I use the term "radical groups." In this case I would also prefer the term "Islamist" over "Islamic" groups, because their interpretation of Islam is quite unique. It is not necessarily fundamentalist, but that is the topic for another lecture.

The core perception of the Islamist Arab groups is that they face a global conspiracy against the Islamic world, against Islamic countries, and against the Islamic mind. They fear a plot to implant in Islamic minds (mainly those of youngsters) secularism and heretical ideas. This plot's aim is to induce them to forget Islamic principles and, according to their perception, to lose their backbone—which is not nationalism, communism, socialism, or any other of the imported ideologies from the West, but rather Islam as the only true religion.

Now, mainly after the establishment of Israel and the renaissance of the Islamist groups since the '60's and '70's, this conspiracy came to be viewed as a constant and perhaps eternal struggle between Judaism and Islam. And this struggle cannot be resolved by the creation of one state or another. This is an eternal struggle, which can end only when one of the two sides vanquishes the other. Thus they regard themselves as involved in a constant war where, if I may borrow a phrase from Professor Palazzi, they refer to what the Prophet Muhammad called "the Greater Jihad."

In orthodox Islam this "Greater Jihad" is not the military Jihad, but rather the internal Jihad of every Muslim individual with himself. The Islamists, however, turned the latter into "the Lesser Jihad" and put the military Jihad at the top of their priorities. They justified this perception by stating that in this constant war every true Muslim, and needless to say each member of every Islamist group, must regard himself as a soldier, as belonging first of all to what they call Hizballah—the party of God.

This term, by the way, was not invented in Lebanon in 1982, but appears in the Qur'an. It actually refers to the true believers who are engaged in a permanent struggle with Hizbasheitan—the party of the devil, the infidels. In the past, these were the pagans. Now the heretics, the pagans, have evolved into the Western culture, in alliance with Judaism. So every individual Muslim is facing a conspiracy—a global conspiracy—on a daily basis, every minute of his life. And therefore, he must be not only a part of Hizballah, the party of God, but also a part of Jundalla, the army of God.

Thus, most of the Islamist groups were founded on a semi-military basis, not only in order to fight and to carry out terrorism, but also so that in every circumstance their members will regard themselves as soldiers, and they will be constantly motivated to confront the enemy. This is a struggle between good and evil, light and darkness. Naturally, the presentation of the situation in such eternal terms gives rise to a willingness to carry out violence. Not only suicide terrorism, but violence in general is justified not only by the fact that the Islamists regard Islam as the true religion, but also because they see themselves as exposed to constant dangers from an enemy who is everywhere. This enemy may be an Arab secular leader, the Arab secular environment or society, or, even worse, the representative of modernism.

Actually, at the foundation of Islamist revivalism is an essential fear of the inability to cope with Western modernization. It is for this reason that Western modernization poses a threat. Thus, the West is the enemy.

And as the Islamists see it, in 1948 the West placed Israel right in the middle of the Arab world, in order to disseminate this evil culture—to engage the Muslims in a war of culture rather than military might. It is an attempt to conquer their minds, to remove Islam, their spiritual core, from their minds, and then bring them to their knees. Therefore the struggle against this conspiracy—this terrible enemy—becomes a Jihad or a war of self-defense. They are the ones being attacked. They are not only oppressed, but they are victims of a wholesale attack.

And in a war of self-defense you may use whatever means are at your disposal to fight the enemy—because the enemy represents the Devil. However, the Devil does not appear as some horrible enemy. He is very attractive. He lurks everywhere. He is behind every corner. He knows all the tricks of how to control the mind. In such a sophisticated war you not only can, but also must use whatever means you have to fight.

The result is the Islamist groups, and in our case, Hamás and Hizballah, who regard themselves as those who stand in the frontlines of the struggle against this global conspiracy, because they are fighting Israel. They are waging battle against the primary enemy. And therefore they must use the extreme method of suicide terrorism. This is not only meant to vanquish the enemy, but also to introduce into the fight another element, the sociological element.

Stereotyping as justification for suicide terrorism

This sociological element is characteristic of Islamist terrorism in general, and of suicide terrorism in particular. The enemy is perceived as a coward. The enemy is, on the one hand, very strong, stronger than are the Islamists, who are the weaker factor in this equation. But the enemy is also a coward. Why is he perceived as a coward? Because Western society and Israeli Jewish society are primarily made up of pleasure seekers who fear death and suicide. These fears, combined with the quest for "the good life," are viewed as the basic tenets of Western culture. And so, the Muslims or the members of the Islamist groups must not only fight the enemy, but show him that they are truly brave, because the ultimate bravery and heroism lie in seeking out death, thus showing the enemy as cowards and themselves as heroes.

The willingness to die

I would like to conclude with a factor that is one of the consequences of these perceptions of the struggle between Islam and the West, or Islamism versus the Western culture, or Islamism versus Judaism. In most cases, and I refer here mainly to those involving Hamas and the Palestinian Islamic Jihad in the Palestinian arena, it has been very easy to recruit volunteers for these operations. Not only is it extremely easy to find people willing to die, but in many cases of suicide terrorism the volunteers were recruited for the operation only a week or a few days before the operation.

There is no battalion of volunteers constantly training to commit suicide. But there exists the constant *willingness* to commit suicide. From time to time members of Hamas even recruit their own family members—cousins, for example. They are influenced by their perception of the ultimate level of the struggle against this conspiracy, these terribly brutal enemies they are facing. Thus the organizations succeed in recruiting these people very easily.

Although I refer mainly to the Palestinian arena, the same holds true of Islamist radical groups elsewhere. In the case of the assassination of the late President Sada'at, the killers were captured alive, although they had been certain prior to the operation that they were going to die. So although this operation did not meet all of the precise criteria for a suicide operation, they were still sure that they were going to be killed. The three individuals who carried out the operation with Haled Islambuli were recruited on the First of October, 1981, only four days prior to the operation. So again, here we see what the Egyptian sociologist described as prevalent in many cases in the Arab world, not only in the Palestinian arena.

Conclusion

The Islamist activity is highly successful, and must be fought or confronted by what Professor Palazzi calls "Islamic Moderation." But it must be confronted mainly by using its own weapons—the appeal to the spirit. Personally, I do not believe that there exist technical means to fight these operations. The only way to counter the influence of these groups is to target the social and religious foundations on which they have built their successes.

Characteristics of Suicide Terrorism Worldwide

Session Chairman: Prof. Martha Crenshaw,
Wesleyan University, U.S.A.

Suicide Terrorism in Sri Lanka and India

Dr. Rohan Gunaratna

Research Associate, Center for the Study of Terrorism and Political Violence, University of St. Andrews, Scotland

I would like to give here an illustrated presentation on the phenomenon of suicide terrorism in Sri Lanka and India. Some of my visuals may be disturbing, but unless you observe the process of a suicide bomber approaching the target, the tension, and the aftermath of the blast, I believe that it is difficult to understand the reality of suicide operations.

First, allow me to give you the background, the context, of my presentation. Sri Lanka is an island in the south of India. Seventy-four percent of its population is composed of Sinhalis, while the Tamils constitute about 12.5% of the total population of the Sri-Lankan people.

The only group that conducts suicide operations in Sri Lanka is "The Liberation Tigers of Tamil Eelam," also known as the LTTE, or in the Western world, the "Tamil Tigers." The group was formed in 1972 and launched its first suicide operation in 1987. In 1981 several senior members of this organization were arrested. In consequence, a decision was made at that time for every member of the organization to carry a cyanide capsule on his person. The capsule contains potassium or sodium cyanide packed in a small glass tube. When an LTTE fighter is injured, or if he is on the verge of capture, he will consume this potassium cyanide capsule. He must bite the capsule, which is enclosed in glass. The glass cuts the gum, and the potassium cyanide inside the tube will then make direct contact with the bloodstream. The fighter will suffer a few convulsions and die.

India and the LTTE

The history of the Sri-Lankan conflict between 1983 and 1987 indicates that Sri Lanka maintained very poor relations with its northern neighbor, India. At that time Sri Lanka was under Western influence, and had very strong economic and political ties with Europe and North America. It also enjoyed very close ties with Israel during that period.

India was very much within the Soviet sphere of influence. It had a treaty of cooperation with the Soviet Union. India's perception was that Sri Lanka was being used as a launching pad to destabilize India. As a result, the Liberation Tigers of Tamil Eelam, as well as some other groups, were based in the southern part of India and operated from inside that country.

But in 1987 all this began to change; the Indian and Sri-Lankan governments signed a treaty for peace and cooperation. In consequence of this agreement, 100,000 Indian soldiers were deployed in Sri Lanka to maintain peace. The Liberation Tigers of Tamil Eelam then declared war on the Indian Government and on the Indian peacekeeping force. The Indian peacekeeping force was stationed in Sri Lanka from July 1987 until March 1990. In March 1990 the Indian peacekeeping force withdrew.

During that period of time a new Sri-Lankan President came to power. This president initiated peace talks with the Tamil Tigers. The peace talks were only a tactical move on the part of the Liberation Tigers of Tamil Eelam; however, the Sri-Lankan President failed to recognize this fact, and he insisted on the withdrawal of the Indian peacekeeping force. About three months after the withdrawal of the peacekeeping force, the Liberation Tigers of Tamil Eelam resumed their war.

The LTTE's suicide attacks

I have already mentioned that the potassium cyanide capsule was introduced in 1981, while the first suicide attack occurred in 1987. This first suicide operation was conducted under very interesting circumstances, and I believe that it is important to be familiar with the circumstances behind every suicide operation. For if we understand the context of each and every suicide operation, this will serve as the key to how we can find ways to change the behavior of terrorist and guerrilla organizations.

In May 1987, about a month before the suicide operation, Sri-Lankan troops conducted a large-scale operation to recover an area called the Jaffna peninsula. The areas that are marked in red are where Sri-Lankan Tamils live. Of course there are Sri-Lankan Tamils living in the southern area of the Island and also in the capital of Colombo, but the majority of the Sri-Lankan Tamils reside in the northeast. The Liberation Tigers of Tamil Eelam suffered a series of humiliating defeats in combat. Their pride was wounded and they sought revenge.

The organization had previously attacked military camps by sending explosives-laden trucks into the camps, from which the drivers would jump out just before detonation. These attacks were not particularly effective, as the trucks did not usually reach the intended targets. There were also difficulties with the detonation.

Eventually, one of the LTTE drivers volunteered to serve as a suicide bomber. The first suicide attack was conducted by a man named Miller. In this suicide operation, 16 soldiers were killed and 22 were injured. Miller was posthumously raised to the rank of captain by the LTTE in recognition of his act.

During the deployment of the Indian peacekeeping force between July 1987 and March 1990, there were no suicide operations. There are various reasons for this. In order to mount a suicide operation, several elements are required. One prerequisite is that there must be surveillance; the target and the level of security must be carefully monitored. Another is that in-depth research must be conducted to ensure that the operation is successful. And third is the need for a solid support network to house the suicide bomber, the arms, ammunition, explosives, the support team, and the surveillance team.

The Indian peacekeeping force denied the Liberation Tigers of Tamil Eelam the opportunity to mount surveillance and to have safe houses in some of the critical areas where the Indian army was deployed in force. This is the main reason that there were no suicide operations during the deployment of the IPKF (the Indian Peacekeeping Force) during that period. However, immediately after the withdrawal of the peacekeeping force, there were a number of suicide operations.

The LTTE's suicide bombings

There have been three periods of peace talks between the Government of Sri Lanka and the Liberation Tigers of Tamil Eelam. In each instance, during the peace talks the Liberation Tigers of Tamil Eelam infiltrated the capital of Colombo. This is a very central point, because when there are peace talks it is very important to monitor the formation of these sleeper-cells, and the transport of arms and ammunition to certain areas. The level of security tends to drop, as does the level of attention paid by security personnel to the organization.

The peace talks broke down in July 1990. On 2 March 1991, the Tamil Tigers launched their first suicide attack in the capital of Colombo, killing the Minister of Defense.

Suicide devices

I have mentioned that the first attack took place on March 2, 1991. The second attack was launched on June 21, 1991, when the Tamil Tigers destroyed the headquarters of the Joint Operations Command, the headquarters of the Sri-Lankan security forces. Once again, the assault took the form of a suicide bomb in a vehicle.

There are several types of suicide devices. One is the vehicle improvised with an explosive device, where explosives are fitted to a vehicle and the driver activates the switch. The second type of suicide device is what is called a suicide body suit. This is essentially a denim vest, equipped with explosives and two switches. One switch is for arming the device and another is for triggering the device. The idea for this suicide device came from the jacket that Tamil Tigers generally wore, which featured ammunition pouches.

An obvious question is: Who supplied the explosives? Initially the organization acquired explosives by attacking Sri-Lankan police and military targets. However, in 1994, during the second round of peace talks with the Sri-Lankan Government, the headquarters of the Liberation Tigers of Tamil Eelam in London negotiated with the U.K.rainian Government to purchase 60 tons of powerful explosives. This purchase included 50 tons of TNT and 10 tons of RDX, also known as hexogen. The LTTE formed a consultant company in the U.K.raine called "Euro U.K.rainian Consultancy Company," which served as a front organization for the group. The company procured consignments of explosives using false end-user certificates signed by the Secretary of Defense of Bangladesh. A Tamil Tiger ship named *Sweeny* left the Black Sea port of Nickolev with the consignment of explosives, passed the port of Garves in Turkey, came around Africa into Sri Lanka and unloaded this consignment of explosives. According to technical specialists in the capabilities of terrorist groups, this particular consignment may last for another ten years at least.

Another variation on suicide bombs is called "suicide shots," and makes use of steel ball bearings. During the explosion, these ball bearings will move at a very high speed and destroy whatever lies in their path.

Yet another variation is the belt-bomb, and is also worn in the abdominal area. This device also uses steel ball bearings.

In March 1990, the Indian peacekeeping force withdrew. Now the Indian peacekeeping force was first deployed in Sri Lanka on the basis of an agreement signed between the Sri-Lankan President and the Prime Minister of India, Rajiv Gandhi. When the peacekeeping force withdrew, Rajiv Gandhi was no longer in office, but was running in an election that would have brought him to power in May 1991. However, the Tamil Tigers did not want Rajiv Gandhi to become Prime Minister, because the organization had suffered severely under the Indian peacekeeping force. So they decided to assassinate Rajiv Gandhi on the eve of the election campaign.

Suicide operations after the withdrawal of the peacekeeping force

After May 1990, a number of variations were introduced in LTTE suicide operations. The first variation occurred when the naval commander of Sri Lanka visited India to discuss naval cooperation. The main supply route for the Sri-Lankan Tamil Tigers runs very close to India. Naval cooperation between Sri Lanka and India could potentially hamper or disrupt the arrival of these supplies. The Sri-Lankan Navy commander visited India to hold discussions with his counterpart, and within a week of his arrival the Sri-Lankan Tamil Tigers staged a suicide operation.

This attack was very different from previous ones. In this instance, a Tamil Tiger wearing a suicide jacket and riding a motorcycle drew up to the Navy commander's vehicle and leaped onto the vehicle of the Navy commander. A backup vehicle was following the Navy commander. However, there was nothing that the backup vehicle could do. The commander was killed, as were his bodyguard and driver.

One of the individuals who initiated peace talks with the Tamil Tigers was Sri-Lankan President Premadasa. The suicide bomber who killed President Premadasa had infiltrated the President's household while the talks were in progress. He was in and out of the President's household regularly. So you can see that there was a grave failure in intelligence, and completely inadequate security. As the President left to address a press conference on May 1, 1993, the suicide bomber approached him. As the attacker approached, the President's valet in fact greeted the suicide bomber, because the latter had befriended the valet.

The reason the President was targeted was because he had been demanding that Sri-Lankan security forces reoccupy the Jaffna peninsula, which was occupied by the Tamil Tigers at the time. The Tamil Tigers did not want the Jaffna peninsula to be occupied by the Sri-Lankan military forces. This was the single reason behind the assassination. For two years the Sri-Lankan security forces did not recover the Jaffna Peninsula, and it was only in 1995 that the Sri-Lankan security forces launched an operation to recover the peninsula. To preempt that operation, the Tamil Tigers destroyed oil storage facilities in Colombo. These were the facilities that were fueling Sri-Lankan aircraft, Sri-Lankan vehicles, and Sri-Lankan naval craft. Six suicide bombers were used in this operation.

At the height of the operation to recover the Jaffna peninsula, the Sri-Lankan Tamil Tigers also attacked the central bank. This assault took place in January 1996. The U.S. State Department classified it as the worst act of international terrorism of 1996. Eighty-six individuals were killed and 1338 people were injured, including several foreigners. About 100 people lost their eyesight.

The Liberation Tigers of Tamil Eelam experienced a degree of failure when they attacked the central bank. The suicide bomber came in a truck, while a three-wheeler carrying two LTTE fighters was used to provide protection and to escort the suicide bomber to the target. The two LTTE fighters were captured, and later revealed substantial information about the organization's operations. To prevent this from happening again, in all subsequent suicide operations all participants in the operation wore suicide jackets. From then on, multiple suicide bombers were utilized.

Eight suicide bombers were used to destroy the Sri-Lankan World Trade Center. This was a revenge attack launched a week after the U.S. State Department declared the LTTE a terrorist group. Of course, the surveillance for this target had been done a considerable time in advance. There were a number of targets that the LTTE had planned to destroy, but the timing for this target clearly coincided with the Americans' designation of the LTTE as a terrorist group. The LTTE operatives who did not perish in the attack withdrew to a nearby newspaper office and there blew themselves up, killing a number of civilians.

Recent developments

The Sri-Lankan Government had been persistent in endeavoring to make peace with this terrorist group, and were planning to conduct another round of peace negotiations. As a prelude to this round of peace negotiations, they decided to extend autonomy to the northeast region. The main individual behind this development was a Sri-Lankan Tamil and renowned scholar, Dr. Nilan Piruchelmam. Dr. Piruchelmam was targeted by an LTTE suicide attacker while traveling in his vehicle. As his car slowed at a traffic light, the suicide bomber approached the vehicle and detonated his explosives, killing Dr. Piruchelmam.

I would like to make two final points. One is that no country has witnessed such a great number of suicide operations in such a short period of time as Sri Lanka. No country has lost as many leaders as Sri Lanka has in such a short period of time, and this is due solely to suicide terrorism attacks.

As we see it, this is a phenomenon that is spreading. It represents a major threat that must be addressed through skilled intelligence and highly effective preventive and reactive security measures.

Suicide Terrorism in Turkey:
The Workers' Party of Kurdistan

Professor Dogu Ergil

Chairman, Department of Political Behavior, Ankara University, Turkey

The PKK is an offshoot of the leftist movement—a movement that had a major impact on Turkish politics throughout the '60's and '70's. But constrained by severe official pressure and confronted by Turkish nationalists and religious movements nurtured by the "establishment," left-wing Kurds increasingly relied on their ethnicity as a force for political mobilization. Ethnic difference became the ideological fuel of their politics as the power of the left was curtailed by two military coups in 1971 and 1980, and by its inability to present itself as a legitimate project for modernization and development.

The PKK was founded by a group of young Kurdish citizens of Turkey in the village of Urfa in 1978. Its Marxist-Leninist ideology made it easy for its leaders to adopt armed struggle as a legitimate political form. The group soon came to be known as Apacu, after its leader "APO," short for Abdullah Ocalan. Only a few living members of the original group remain, because they were either liquidated by Ocalan himself or killed in action.

After an initial phase of organization, recruitment and vying with other Kurdish organizations for dominance, the PKK moved to Syria and the Beka'a Valley of Lebanon to escape pressure on Kurdish organizations in the wake of the 1980 coup in Turkey. It was in these locations that the PKK grew, organized internationally and trained in guerrilla tactics and sabotage. Apart from Syria, which hosted the bulk of the organization and its leadership, the PKK found other allies in the Middle East and supporters further afield.

In August of 1984, after years of preparation and training, the PKK launched its first attack on official state targets inside Turkey.

By then, in the wake of the 1980 coup, the ensuing military administration had wiped out all legal and illegal Kurdish organizations in Turkey, and the PKK emerged as the dominant force on the Kurdish political scene. Until its decision to abandon armed struggle against Turkey in February 2000, the PKK fought against the Turkish State and non-PKK Kurds alike. Its armed struggle led to the loss of more than 35,000 soldiers, policemen, and civilians, including innocent women and children, as well as many PKK fighters, both men and women.

The PKK as an organization

What started as a youthful, radical, ethnic organization with several dozen men of rural origin burgeoned into an international outfit with a well-trained militia that had swelled to 20,000 men and women by the 1990's. With its wide logistic links and range of political supporters, it reached and influenced several hundred thousand people. Many of its supporters would never have backed the cruel, Stalinist-type regime the PKK would have established. However, after living under martial law for more than half the republic's history, denied cultural freedom, including public expression of their cultural identity, and feeling trapped in one of Turkey's most isolated and impoverished regions, some of the Kurds found their present status no better than the painful struggle offered by the PKK. They took consolation in the fact that the PKK was composed of their own people, and had raised the flag of rebellion against the conditions that were weighing them down. Moreover, the PKK opposed the traditional feudal and tribal formations that divided the Kurdish population, and which significantly contributed to its backwardness. The PKK rebellion was not only against official repression; it was also against the Kurdish predicament, characterized by traditionalism, feudalism, tribalism and backwardness. Its targets were both the Turkish "establishment," which failed to transform the backward region and population of the southeast, and the traditional Kurdish elite, which oppressed the local Kurds and sided with the "establishment" in order to preserve its privileged position.

Given this background, the PKK may be described as:

1. *Armed* (hence illegal)

2. *Ethnic*

3. *Nationalist* – Although the group started as a Marxist-Leninist organization, it always harbored nationalistic aims and sentiments. Its ultimate goal—unlike other Kurdish organizations elsewhere in the Middle East—was to unite all Kurds in a larger Kurdistan, with water and petroleum sources, as well as access to the sea. After recognizing the fruitlessness of his Marxist orientation for his recruits, who were predominantly of peasant origin, and the West's reluctance to support a Stalinist organization, the PKK leader dropped the Marxist-Leninist label from the organization's charter in the second half of the 1990's.

4. *Absolutist* – Its rules were tantamount to religious dogma. Disobedience meant execution. Only the leader made rules; rewards and punishment were his prerogative.

5. *Hierarchical* – The organization had only one leader. There were no second or third men in the chain of command. Everyone reported directly to the leader and everything he said and did was law. There was no vetoing mechanism. The PKK was born in a tribal atmosphere, which was reflected in its structure. It was built and functioned as a political tribe. The second important source of political influence on the PKK was the Turkish State, and that too contributed to the organization's hierarchical structure, as Turkey's Jacobean character (administration and mobilization from above) was largely adopted by the PKK. The attempt to create a Kurdish nation from a divided and disorganized Kurdish population with linguistic (Za Za – Kurmanci), religious (Sunni - Alevi), and regional differences, was reminiscent of the Kemalist tradition of "revolution and mobilization from above."

6.   *Secular* – The PKK did not rely on religion except in passing, or when it was a convenient tool to win over traditional local people. Neither the pronounced secularism of its leader nor its blend of Marxist and ethno-nationalist ideology left much room for religion. In fact, it was the government that revived religious feelings in order to replace ethnic consciousness with Islamic brotherhood. Later, the National Salvation Party (now the Virtue Party) used religion as a rallying point against both Turkish and Kurdish nationalism.

The impact of the nature of the PKK on its members

The PKK recruited most of its militia from the villages and towns of southeast Anatolia. It is basically a rural organization. Some of the more prominent members have had an unsuccessful urban experience—including the leader, who is a college dropout from the Faculty of Political Science, Ankara University, where the author teaches. Recruits from Turkey's urban centers and European cities are children of Kurdish immigrants. However, few people of urban background with higher education were able to rise to positions of leadership in the organization, partly because fighting is its basic vocation, and partly because the leader did not allow anyone with higher qualifications than his own to gain prominence. The organization's rural character has always influenced its basic strategy of fighting for land rather than for basic rights, principles, or democratic ideals and institutions. Moreover, it has come out openly against intellectuals and intellectualism, stifling such members in the organization, and in Kurdish politics as a whole.

The rural character of the PKK has another important bearing on its rank and file, who have long been dependent on feudal lords, tribal chieftains or traditional heads of extended families. In the organization, this dependency is transferred to the omnipotent leader. Ocalan is no different from Saddam Hussein or Hafez al-Asad in his leadership style. The transformation of his cruelty into unchallenged leadership created a formidable charisma, which still holds sway over some people despite his incarceration in Turkey since December 1998.

Ocalan's lasting impact on his organization is reflected in the PKK's decision to elect him again as party head at the organization's Seventh Congress—which met in a cave in north Iraq close to the Turkish-Iranian border—in February 2000. Although he is in a Turkish prison and condemned to death, the organization still considers him its leader because there has never been an alternative, and everything revolves around a personality cult. This fact is central to the indoctrination of the group's members.

Constant movement in difficult, mountainous terrain and living in the countryside with little contact with the outside world has made the organization into the only social milieu for its members. PKK members have become dependent on the organization and on their leader to tell them what to do, how to live, and how to die.[1] Their youth and rural background has not afforded opportunities for them to emerge as independent personalities. The organization definitely carried this phenomenon to the extreme, leaving its members no room for privacy or individualism.

The PKK identifies itself as a warrior organization.[2] Its declared enemy is the Turkish Republic (TR), which stands accused of oppression and colonialism. The concept of the colonization of the Kurdish territories was developed by Abdullah Ocalan as part of a Marxist analysis designed to legitimize the armed struggle, and the PKK has rationalized its armed struggle as an anti-colonial war against the TR. This rationale enabled the organization to affect a kind of *moral disengagement* from all acts of violence directed against official or unofficial targets declared to be either actually or symbolically related to the "enemy."

Obviously, colonialism was not a characteristic of the Republic of Turkey, but repressing cultural diversity was. Public

---

[1] Jerrold M. Post, "Group and Organizational Dynamics of International Terrorism: Implications for Counter-terrorist Policy" in *Contemporary Research in Terrorism*, P. Wilkinson and A.M. Steward eds., (Aberdeen University Press, 1987).

[2] Wilfred R. Bion, *Experiences in Groups,* (London: Tavistock, 1961).

manifestations of any particularistic group expression, be it ideological or cultural, were perceived as a threat to the unity of the Turkish nation. This narrow ethnic definition of nationhood (although officially denied) left no room for other ethnic, cultural, and religious interpretations or expressions that ran counter to the official line. The collision between the incipient Kurdish nationalism spearheaded by the PKK and the Turkish nationalism adopted as the ideology of nation-building was inevitable. Official discontent took the form of state negligence and persecution. Frustration emanating from Kurds inability to identify themselves as such in the public domain led to charges of victimization. These feelings of frustration were reinforced by a sense of deprivation, isolation, backwardness, and poverty. The state was blamed for all these failings. Any attack on its institutions, personnel, or symbolic supporters was both a rebellion against injustice and a cry for help to ease the adverse conditions, which the Kurds, represented by the PKK, were enduring.

The PKK saw its role as the deliverance of the Kurds of Turkey from the subjugation of an unjust and "alien" state, as well as from their own backwardness. So Kurdish suffering could end only by breaking away from the Turkish state and everything affiliated with it. There is no detail in this battle cry, and it leaves key questions unanswered. What will follow armed struggle? What kind of political system and economic model will be established? How much freedom will individuals have?

Exaggeration of the richness of the area (Turkey, Iran, Iraq and Syria, where the Kurdish enclaves are situated), with its abundant supplies of water, oil and other natural resources, as well as access to the sea, recurs in PKK rhetoric. Although the claims are not realistic, they chart a real map for the struggle and set a goal, and demand total commitment to the armed struggle until the goal is reached. Everything that contributes to the realization of the goal is legitimate, including killing and dying.

Fighting and dying for the exalted cause—liberation of the Kurds and creation of an independent Kurdistan—are as binding as holy scriptures for PKK members, whose lives have not seen much else to which they could commit themselves with such devotion.

Their withdrawal into the organization is not a great sacrifice, because their daily lives, on the whole, do not carry much meaning.

PKK membership, as in other groups with a high degree of emotional investment in an "exalted mission," redefines the lives of the young, rural and small-town members. It prioritizes their values, placing membership and obedience to directives at the top of the list.[3] It also unites the group around the leadership and group rules and directives. This situation further isolates the members from society at large and sanctifies group norms and solidarity.

Group pressure under these circumstances becomes all-encompassing. Members' judgments and behavior are strongly influenced by the omnipotent leader and the forces of group dynamics. Any other source or form of morality is superseded by the morality of the organization. In this moral order, the member of the group is seen as an innocent victim. The destruction of the enemy responsible for the group's problems is not only a duty, but also a moral imperative.[4]

The extraordinary conditions PKK fighters have to confront—incessant battles, constant fleeing, hiding in caves and caverns, sharing everything that is in short supply except death, crossing borders into foreign lands—has made the group a material and social haven, outside of which there is nowhere to go. Group pressure in such an organization is all-important. Any violation of group norms and orders means death. Violence is not only a way of achieving group aims; it also irons out deviance and maintains discipline.

This Spartan lifestyle obfuscates real life, and makes the group the center and main focus of members' lives. Dying becomes less important than being outside the group. Excessive risk-taking becomes a routine phenomenon. Irrespective of other forces, the organization seems stronger than it actually is. Group morality is

---

[3] David Rapaport, "Sacred Terror," in *Origins of Terrorism*, ed. by Walter Reich (Washington D.C.: (Woodrow Wilson Center Press, 1998), p.129.

[4] Jerrold M. Post, "Terrorist Psycho-logic" in *ibid*, pp. 33,34.

never questioned or challenged; the "humanness" of the enemy is never considered. The enemy is constantly demonized while even the cruelest group acts are perceived as right, just, or innocent[5] because the "cause" is right.

Once it is accepted that the rules of the group are the only way of life, the member becomes dependent, and can be ordered to do anything, without question. The leader's charisma and unchallenged position, as well as the dynamics of the group, dictate this. Violence as a basic form of political activity becomes a means through which to satisfy the group's quest for achievement. The more violent the member is, the more he or she is rewarded, because through his/her action the group promotes its aims. Hatred for the enemy cultivated during the member's training, as well as feelings of revenge, further sharpen the member's tendency towards violence.

As long as the group possesses the capacity to employ violence effectively, it will try to do so collectively. However, as its capacity to inflict damage on the enemy diminishes, it may call upon individual members to make the ultimate sacrifice. Suicide attacks or suicide terrorism may be one of the calls the organization's leaders make upon its members. In the case of the PKK, such a call came to the public's attention for the first time after the organization's Fifth congress, held in north Iraq in the summer of 1995.[6]

Suicide attacks perpetrated by the PKK

Suicide is not a favored way of death in Turkey due to the basic tenets of Islam, the majority religion. Nevertheless, there is a cultural infrastructure for the readiness to die that emanates from two sources. The first is the nationalistic-chivalric ethos of the warrior. Turks and Kurds, two peoples that have shared a common history for a thousand years, do not differ in this respect. They are

---

[5] Irvin L. Jannis, *Victims of Groupthink,* (Boston: Houghton-Mifflin, 1972).

[6] *Milliyet,* 28.7.1997.

ready die for exalted causes, the ultimate one being defense of the country. It is not surprising that in order to create an imaginary Kurdistan, the PKK leader had to declare the Turkish Republic a colonial power. Thus, the organization's anti-colonial struggle would be to liberate Kurdistan. The second source is the religious concept of "shadat" or martyrdom in a state of war. These two influences reinforce each other and prepare the ground for readiness to sacrifice oneself in a collective struggle waged for higher ideals.

However, this readiness is not the same as the act of "seeking to die."[7] A scrutiny of PKK suicide bombings reveals that the PKK leadership directly ordered all of them. According to reports, none of the candidates, except one, volunteered. They were hand-picked and oriented for their mission. What is asked of the selected persons is to carry their struggle to a higher level of effectiveness. Their chivalry is praised and they are offered a distinguished place in the history of the movement.

It appears that the PKK's suicide bombing is a continuum that involves:

1. *An organization.* In this case it was a very hierarchical, closely knit and leader-oriented group that could order anything of its members and expect compliance.

2. *Charismatic leadership.* The PKK's leader was next to God, and he created and led the organization until the end. He was the founder, organizer, ideologue and commander in chief.

3. *Suitable culture.* The Kurdish society from which the PKK drew its manpower and cultural values was primarily rural. The traditions of chivalry and armed rebellion, combined with a fascination with firearms, kept a fighting spirit aflame. Tribal divisions created a conflict-ridden society with virtually every tribe against the others, making for frequent vendettas. Moreover, religion makes it easy to die for collectively- or religiously-valued ends.

---

[7] Gene Lester and David Lester, *Suicide: the Gamble With Death,* (Englewood Cliffs, N.J.: Prentice-Hall, 1971).

4. *Indoctrination*. The PKK's indoctrination of its members is based on praising valor and rebellion against oppression and victimization. Readiness to die for salvation is further reinforced by the exaltation of selected suicide bombers to the rank of cultural heroes. These persons are asked to prove their commitment to the cause and the organization. They are made to believe that they have been specially selected because of their personal qualities, and that they will change the course of history. They are also told that they will set an example for those who come after them. Therefore, they will become leaders to the living as well as secure a martyr's place for themselves in heaven. Those who are selected are isolated for some time to experience the effects of excommunication if they hesitate. One of the selected members who refused was executed in front of another who was offered the "honor." Another who refused was turned in to the police as she planned her escape from the organization. It appears that a mix of psychological reinforcement, group pressure, and coercion was used in the orientation of suicide bombers of the PKK.

5. *Situational factors*. The PKK had never previously ordered or endorsed suicidal missions by its members, except in prison. PKK members who had been serving long-term prison sentences went on hunger strikes when their demands to be treated as POWs were not met or when they lost faith in getting out early. It was only in these hunger strikes that some PKK members died. Later, PKK sympathizers in Western Europe tried to burn themselves in public out of desperation, when their leader was captured and jailed in Turkey (February 1999). They felt indignant and defeated. He represented all they stood and hoped for. He was the ultimate rebel who fought against all the odds. Maybe the majority of his non-combatant supporters had always believed in their heart of hearts that he would not make it; but he kept the Kurdish spirit alive and made the world aware of Kurdish grievances. He had been the unrivaled communicator on their behalf. Now that this voice was stifled and the course

of events dramatically altered when Ocalan admitted defeat and the fallacy of armed insurrection, the organization and its cause lost their relevance. Now Ocalan began to advocate a striving for democracy in cooperation with the demonized enemy, the state.

The protest suicides, however, did not cause any other deaths. Nor were the hunger strikes and self-immolations staged after Ocalan's detainment in Italy and imprisonment in Turkey individual acts, but rather a result of concerted decision and action by the group. It is reported that when the Turkish government appealed to the Italian authorities for Ocalan's extradition to Turkey, 22 PKK members in Turkish prisons set themselves on fire in protest against it. According to official figures, 22 PKK members burned themselves on 21 different occasions. Five of them died, while the rest of them were rescued and treated.[8] Ocalan responded immediately by saying, "I categorically reject self-immolation. I strongly suggest that they should refrain from setting themselves on fire. If there is anything to burn it is not our sacred lives but individuals and institutions. They stand before us. Let us prepare for [to burn] them. I am talking about serious preparations." (Ocalan's Med-TV address on Dec. 13, 1998).

In another interview on Dec. 25, 1998, Ocalan said, "those who explode the bombs wrapped around themselves in a manner to harm innocent civilians [meaning largely officials] will explode them in crowds that support this fascist government in opposition to the invasion [of our land]. There will be hundreds of explosions. Turkey has to know this… now, I can hardly stop them. But, I may not be able to stop them tomorrow; it is not my responsibility to do so anyway."

Situational factors that led to the advent of suicide bombings became evident in 1995. In hindsight, the Turkish security forces

---

[8] Statistics compiled by the Directory of Counter-terrorism and Operations of the General Directorate of Security, Ministry of Interior, cited by Kemal Karademir, "Intihar Bombacilari," *Polis Bilimleri Dergisi,* (Ankara, Turkey), 1:4 (1999), p.14.

failed to contain PKK violence throughout the 1980's. They were unprepared to deal with organized crime and ethno-nationalist insurrection that covered a large region and involved thousands more combatants over the border. Their experience in monitoring and exterminating urban leftist movements led them to miscalculate in their approach to rural-based, widespread ethnic problems. Unqualified repression enabled the PKK to win more recruits. The untrained soldiers initially proved ineffective in fighting the rural guerrillas, who had been training in their camps for years. Lack of essential equipment (like night-vision capability, attack helicopters and surveillance instruments) also contributed to the inefficiency of security forces. Lastly, a failure to establish alliances with local communities for support and local intelligence networking exacerbated the confusion and inefficiency.

This, however, changed in the 1990's. The PKK was contained at first and then forced to retreat. Hot pursuit into northern Iraq became a nearly perfect drill for the Turkish army. Constant diplomatic pressure on the CIS, Syria, and Iran, and the threat of war directed against the latter, made it harder for countries to support the PKK openly. Drastic measures imposed through martial law led to the evacuation of nearly two thousand villages and smaller scatter-settlements in order to disrupt logistical support for the PKK.

Beginning in 1994, the main strategy of the PKK, which can be described as "gaining physical control of a piece of land and declaring itself the legitimate political representative of the people living on it," began to fail. Statistics show a declining trend of PKK effectiveness in terms of offensive activities. PKK activities peaked in 1993, with 4,198 "incidents," as they are officially known. These ranged from open armed confrontation with security forces to surprise attacks, bombings, mining, road-blocking, kidnapping, armed robbery and illegal demonstrations. (The often-seen Middle-East-style car-bombings have never been perpetrated in Turkey by the PKK.)

PKK activities decreased by 15.2 percent to 3,538 "incidents" in 1994, and this downward trend continued in 1995, with terrorist activities declining by 38.1 percent to 2,200. In 1996, they declined by a further 10.1 percent to 1,976, and in 1997, by 26.3 percent to 1,456. In early 1999, the number of illegal "incidents" throughout the country reported as PKK activity was 1,218—and most of these were distributing handbills and organizing illegal meetings.[9] In 1998, the organization declared that it had ceased hostilities against the Republic of Turkey at the behest of its leader, Abdullah Ocalan, who ordered his militia to leave Turkey. In a dramatic move, the PKK also dropped the word Kurdistan from its name and those of subordinate organizations, relinquishing its claim to territory and any form of sovereignty over it in February 2000.

Still, until Ocalan's eviction from Syria and his ill-fated shuttling adventure in Europe and Africa (which ended in Kenya with his arrest and extradition to Turkey in February 1999), the PKK found itself squeezed in every corner of Turkey, as well as abroad. The level of desperation was evident in its leader's radio and television releases.[10] There was a dramatic move to reverse the downward trend in terrorist efficiency and dwindling morale. A preliminary decision by the Fifth Congress in 1995 was put into effect after an affirmative action plan (adopted by the Fourth Congress) took effect in March 1996.[11]

---

[9] *Ibid*, p.3.

[10] Med-TV was a PKK creation, broadcasting from Europe in two languages: Turkish and Kurdish. It bought time from different corporations with access to satellite service. Under hot legal pursuit of the Turkish government, it had to change locations from which it transmitted its programs. Britain and Belgium were two of these temporary bases.

[11] *"Suicide Attacks,"* an information brief issued by the Directorate of Counter-terrorism and Operations of the General Directorate of Security, dated May 7, 1997. In this "note", there are references to PKK documents confiscated in September 1995 near Bitlis. There are long evaluations of reasons for the immobility of the organization and its failure to implement more effective ways of influencing public opinion. The clues of impending dramatic acts are also found in the documents.

Other factors that paved the way for suicide attacks included severance of PKK groups from one another due to effective government surveillance and pursuit, defection of personnel sent to recruit new manpower in the cities, and difficulties in motivating new warriors and supporters in the face of defeat. The PKK needed to shock its adherents and supporters with examples of ultimate loyalty and sacrifice.

Moreover, the PKK needed continuing international support, in the form of pressure on Turkey to recognize it as a legitimate representative of the Kurds in Turkey. What could be more effective in demonstrating how desperate they were to state their case and to be taken seriously than self-destruction? This strategy was also directed at the government and people of Turkey as a warning of what the PKK was capable of if its case was not taken seriously.

It was in this atmosphere that the PKK leader and other leading members began to defend the notion of "extraordinary" retaliation against "the enemy." The peak of suicide terrorism was the four-month period between Ocalan's arrest in Kenya and imprisonment in Turkey in February 1999, and his trial that ended in a verdict of capital punishment on June 29, 1999. Immediately after his arrest, PKK guerrilla commanders such as Cemal Bayik and Osman Ocalan issued threats on television (Med-TV, 1 and 2 March 1999). Cemal Bayik said, "The youth of Kurdistan must prove that they are APO's *fedayeen.*"[12] Osman Ocalan, Abdullah's brother, said, "It is time to make the enemy pay for its deeds. Fedayeen of the PKK will rock Turkey..." On February 18, the organization issued a declaration addressed "to our nation and international public opinion" on Med-TV, stating that "any form of violence is legitimate in Turkey and Kurdistan... Any and all individuals, institutions and organizations that are hostile to our people, be they civilian or military, are targets of our people."

This inflammatory rhetoric began to take its toll immediately. Starting with an attack on March 4, 1999 in Batman, six suicide

---

[12] One who sacrifices his/her life for a noble cause.

bombings occurred in the space of a month, killing two civilians and wounding thirteen policemen and twenty civilian bystanders.

It seems that both the PKK and its leader wanted to intimate that if Ocalan were executed, they might abandon their basic strategy of selective violence against official targets, and engage in indiscriminate terrorism for the sake of vengeance. Despite some examples to the contrary, the PKK's main targets have been officials, predominantly in southeast Turkey. This was only to be expected, because they always wanted to preserve the claim of being a "liberation movement" for the Kurdish nation and Kurdistan, which did not really exist. As the creator and liberator of Kurdistan, the PKK had to concentrate its activities on the southeastern provinces with their large Kurdish populations. Even the sites of the suicide bombings, with few exceptions, were the southeastern provinces. However, during Ocalan's trial, evidence and PKK rhetoric suggested that limitless and indiscriminate violence was about to start. But the trial went on, despite the suicide attacks. During this time, three "live bombs," two female, Bahar Ercik and Umut Gulay, and a male, Nebi Kuran, were arrested before carrying out their missions.

The last suicide mission was carried out by the PKK on July 5, 1999, in protest of the death sentence handed down to Ocalan a week earlier. However, after the trial, the whole discourse changed concerning the "Kurdish question."

During the trial, Ocalan apologized to the families of the soldiers who had died in the civil strife. He admitted that armed struggle was the wrong strategy, and he promised to order the PKK militia to cease hostilities against Turkish armed forces, later ordering them to leave Turkey. He confessed to the crimes with which he was charged, and then offered to be an agent of peace. He said Turk and Kurd alike should work together to make the Republic more democratic.

This change of attitude, along with a rapid evaluation at the top of the "establishment" on whether or not Ocalan might be more useful alive than dead, created a new situation. In this atmosphere, Ocalan's own survival began to weigh heavily on him. Given a chance to live, he ordered his organization to stop the violence. Suicide bombings perpetrated by the PKK were called off on July 7, 1999.

Characteristics of PKK suicide attacks

Suicide bombings perpetrated by the PKK started on June 30, 1995, and ended on July 5, 1999. Between these dates, fifteen suicide attacks took place. Six were aborted with the apprehension of the perpetrators while still in the preparatory stage. It is through the interrogation of these would-be bombers that a clearer picture of motivation and the mechanics of preparation emerges. The analysis offered here is based on that data, and is further enriched by the investigative work of security and intelligence officers on the backgrounds of deceased bombers.[13] According to the data at hand, the targets of the attacks appear to have been top provincial officials, police, or military personnel and installations. The total casualties in fifteen suicide bombings have been six policemen and nine soldiers killed, twenty-eight policemen and forty-seven soldiers wounded, and four civilians killed and sixty-three wounded. Innocent bystanders have been hurt in attacks on official targets because the targets were chosen for maximum effect on the

---

[13] Unfortunately, there are only three written sources on suicide bombings in Turkey, and they all rely on each other without much diversity. It is best, as this essay has done, to analyze factual data obtained from the authorities and build on it. Two of the available sources are written by police officers, the third is a dissertation written by a public administrator in partial fulfillment of requirements to become a district governor (Kaymakam). Starting from the latter, these sources are as follows:

  i)   Taner Tavas, *"Terorizm Baglaminda Intihar Saldirilari,"* a dissertation submitted to the Faculty of Political Science, Ankara University in 1999.
  ii) Necati Alkan, "Teror Orgutlerinin Intihar Eylemlerindeki Psikodinamik Gercekler," *Polis Akademisi Dergisi,* (Nov-Dec., 1977), pp. 8-10.
  iii) Kemal Karademir, op.cit.

public: police stations, automobiles with officials in them, entrances to military installations, and so on.

Of the fourteen suicide attackers, eleven were young women. This point needs to be examined to shed light on the woman's place in rural militant organizations. The Kurdish rural community is very traditional and affords few freedoms to women. There are still multiple marriages. Young women are virtually bought by their husbands for what is ostensibly dowry money. Their place in the family depends on the men, and they are reduced to doing housework, raising the children and contributing to the family sustenance, with little contact with the outside world. Most of them are not sent to school at all, despite the fact that primary education is obligatory. PKK violence towards schools and teachers, who teach children Turkish and thereby "dilute their Kurdishness," has also been a contributing factor to the ignorance of Kurdish children in the last decade and a half.

Trapped in a vise of traditional culture, family tyranny and grinding gender inequality, young Kurdish women began to look to the PKK not only for ethnic liberation, but for their own emancipation as well. The number of female PKK recruits (although there is no reliable figure) is substantial. They have equal status alongside men in the organization, something they could never have enjoyed at any other place or time. They undergo the same political and military training. This sense of equality, reinforced by a strong sense of duty that is larger than life, seems to be conducive to sacrificing a life that had little meaning before. Moreover, the PKK's ethno-nationalistic appeal cut across tribal and religious lines, so members from different cultural backgrounds intermingled. In these circumstances, the loyalty of women to the organization and its leader might well have been even stronger than that of the men. Therefore, it is no wonder that the leadership found it expedient to exploit them, and selected most of its suicide bombers from among women:

1. It was easier to convince women and keep them under control as "chosen" individuals. Moreover, they were

escorted to the site of the bombing by a male companion who represented the organization that honored them.

2.   Women wanted to contribute to the cause as much as the male members of the group. But in actual battlefield conditions their performance could not match that of their male counterparts. Their need for achievement and compensation in other areas was a driving force in their accepting the suicide role. This comes out very clearly in the recorded statements of a deceased "live-bomb," as well as from others arrested before committing the act.

3.   Once they had left the traditional family, they could not return, primarily because they would not have been welcomed. Moreover, being caught as a PKK member was not a preferable option either, unless one became an informer or counter-terrorist in the service of the government.

4.   Women arouse less suspicion from the security forces. They can be equipped with explosives and dressed as though they are pregnant, making male policemen or soldiers less likely to frisk them as they approach the target.

5.   Women who had lost relatives or loved ones in the struggle were ready to take strong action to avenge their loss. Their political family provided an opportunity to take revenge for the members of their biological family—a very important factor in traditional society.

6.   According to oral accounts from arrested male PKK members, women became an increasing burden in hit-and-run tactics and extremely long marches across the mountains. Suicide missions became an effective method for thinning their ranks.[14]

---

[14] Originally a PKK guerrilla, later an informant, Seyfi Demirkiran gave a detailed account of his impression of his years with the organization in a book entitled, *Urperten Itiraflar: PKK ile 3.5 Yil,* (Chilling Revelations: Three and half Years With the PKK), (Istanbul: Turan, 1996).

Apart from the higher number of women among the successful suicide bombers, police suggest that three of the people involved in the six aborted attempts were also women.[15]

The ages of the female perpetrators ranged from 17 to 27. None of them possessed professional skills, and some were high-school dropouts. Most of them came from poor, crowded families.

There are two cases that are worthy of further scrutiny. Leyla Kaplan carried out a suicide bombing at the entrance to the building of the Adana Police Rapid Deployment Force Directorate, killing three policemen and wounding eight officers, a police technician, and three civilian bystanders. She did not volunteer for the mission; far from it. The duty was first offered to another female PKK member, Turkan-Adiyaman, who declined. Her refusal led to her execution in front of Leyla Kaplan, who was then offered the job. She accepted.

Another case is that of Elif Mavis. Born in 1980 in France to an immigrant Kurdish family from the Gercus Township of Batman in southeastern Turkey, she was influenced by PKK propaganda while in high school in the French town of Creil. She received political training in France, Holland, and Germany from PKK operatives. While in Koln she was approached by PKK members to be a live-bomb in Istabul. When she refused, she was subjected to severe pressure and decided to "escape" to Istanbul from Europe. However, she was arrested the moment she set foot in Istanbul airport, on December 30, 1998. The most likely scenario is that the organization turned her in to the authorities, since as a French citizen with no legal liability, she would normally be considered "untouchable."

It seems as though there was a considerable degree of coercion in suicide bombings, because the suicide modus operandi was neither endorsed by the culture nor by the organization's practice

[15] "Information Note" sent to all Province Governors by the Directorate of Counter-terrorism and Operations on February 22, 1999, cited in K. Karademir, *op.cit*, p.11.

before its decline. This raises the question of how the selected suicide bombers were oriented and motivated.

There was one case of voluntary acquiescence to being a live-bomb. Umut Gulay, born in the Viransehif township of Urfa in 1975, in her February 1999 "Progress Report" of what she had done so far, maintained that her loyalty to Ocalan might allow her to accept a suicide mission. She was given the job, and along with her male companions, engaged in surveillance for a planned attack on police or military gatherings in the center of Mus. However, on the appointed day she became frightened, and hid the bombs, which had been wrapped around her. Fleeing from both the organization and police, she was caught on her way to a metropolitan center.[16]

In all other cases, male and female candidates alike were handpicked by the organization for the "heroic act" in the name of anti-colonialism and national liberation. The only available transcript of an audiotape recorded by a live-bomb is that of Leyla Kaplan. Before going to her death, she speaks of giving up her body to the organization and its "cause." She does not, however, mention martyrdom at all. Are there other recorded soundtracks, and, if there are, shouldn't they be made available?

We don't know, because everything related to security is a state secret. But it is doubtful that religion plays any role in suicide bombing. It is my personal opinion that the organization and its cause have in fact replaced the sanctity of religion for its members. Their individuality has melted into a collective organizational entity. Living in the virtual reality of the organizational nexus, shaped by the extraordinary conditions of warfare, has made members identify with the organization more than with any other reality.

This fact is further exacerbated by the isolation of "candidates" for three to six months without giving them any duties. Being without a duty is similar to excommunication in tightly knit

---

[16] Both cases are cited in K. Karademir, *ibid.*, based on police intelligence reports from the provinces in which the events took place.

organizations. Declaring that they have a "special" mission fills the vacuum. The exaltation brings enormous pressure to bear on the candidates. Refusal means excommunication or execution. It is best to accept things, and make of the most of having been "selected" to serve the cause. The recruiting organizations melt away individual egos and forge an *espirit-de-corps* which is utilized in the promotion of selfless acts. This, in short, seems to be the way suicide bombers are produced.[17]

The PKK has never really promised heaven to its suicide bombers. Similarly, it has not emphasized religious motifs or transcendent salvation. But everything that could have been said of the sacred domain has been said of the organization, its leader and its cause. A seemingly secular rhetoric has sacred ramifications for the members. This, along with other aspects of group thinking, has made it possible to sacrifice lives.

Regarding male suicide bombers, it is hard to draw conclusions about their personality profiles. Of the four suicide bombers, two were young, at 18 and 22 respectively. They were uneducated, out of school and had severed all ties with their families. The other two were older at 35 and 40, and were no longer able to keep pace with the stringent demands of rural guerrilla warfare. Of the four men who were arrested before they could carry out their planned attacks, one was 40 years old, while the other three were 18, 22, and 25. The four arrested females ranged in age from 18 to 24.[18]

Except for two incidents in Istanbul and Adana, which harbor large Kurdish enclaves, all suicide attacks have taken place in the southeastern provinces of Turkey, which the PKK claimed to be in the process of liberating. This geographical choice was part of a symbolic effort to delineate the zone, which the organization calls

---

[17] "What Makes a Suicide Bomber?" *Time*, 16.1.1995; Aysegul Aydogan, "Eylemciler Ice Donuk Kisilige Sahip," *Milliyet*, 25.12.1998; also, Nuriye Akman, "Olum Doguran Bomba Kizlar," *Sabah*, serialized article, 9-13 November, 1996.

[18] Calculated from factual data provided by K. Karademir, op. cit., pp. 15-29.

Turkish or northern "Kurdistan." But whatever the PKK's motivation in initiating this most dramatic form of terrorism, the campaign ended as abruptly, in July 1999, as it had started four years earlier. The PKK leadership gave orders to stop the suicide bombings because such actions were putting the life of the captured leader at risk, while he was pleading to be allowed to live—in return for peace. Later, all hostilities ceased on his order. And Ocalan's death sentence will most likely be commuted to life imprisonment when Turkey abolishes capital punishment in the near future.[19]

Regarding the suicide terrorism of the PKK, what started as an executive order ended with another executive initiative. It seems that such acts of violence will no longer emanate from the mainstream PKK. However, splinter groups seeking to distance themselves from the now "docile" organization with its jailed leader could opt for spectacular acts of violence.

The evidence suggests that there are also other groups that could adopt suicide terrorism. Members of the ultra-nationalist group, the "Turkish Revenge Brigade," which was responsible for the shooting of Akin Birdal, President of the Human Rights Association in 1998, threatened to resort to suicide bombings during a live television transmission (Channel D, night of October 11, 1998). A group of Islamic fundamentalists that has organized in Germany under the name of the "Union of Islamic Communities and Associations" claimed to have founded the Federated State of Anatolia (as part of a wider Islamic world entity) a few years ago. A small group with no more than three thousand adherents, they have been seeking to do something spectacular in order to be taken seriously. For example, they plotted an explosive aerial nose-dive into Ataturk's Mausoleum in Ankara on the day of the

---

[19] The Turkish government has bought time by deciding to wait for the decision of the European Court of Justice before the legal procedure is completed. Thus, while holding off public pressure, preparations are being made to lift capital punishment, which is part of the requirements for adapting Turkish law to European legal standards in order to achieve full membership of the European Union.

commemoration of his death, with all top state officials present to pay their respects (November 10, 1988). They tried to rent a plane in Bursa, load it with explosives, and dive into the compound. Ten members of this fanatical group were arrested before they could realize their sinister goal.[20]

Conclusion

Suicide terrorism has no tradition in Turkey. It was introduced by the PKK as a means of reviving its fortunes after its paramilitary effectiveness began to dwindle in the mid-1990's. It reached its peak in the period between Ocalan's arrest in Kenya (February 16, 1999) and his trial in Turkey (May 31-June 29, 1999). The PKK desperately wanted to create the impression that a death sentence on their leader would result in the group's creating havoc throughout Turkey. This ran counter to their basic strategy of territorial control and political representation. However, they felt cornered and were desperate to "break out." Fifteen suicide attacks were carried out. Eleven of the perpetrators were women and four were men.

The PKK used a combination of coercion and motivational techniques facilitated by absolute loyalty to the organization and its leader. Absolute loyalty to the organization was possible mainly because of the rural-traditional character of the population constituting the PKK's social base. Divided along feudal and tribal lines, relatively isolated from society at large and the rest of the world, local Kurds are more aware of their ethnic difference than Kurds living in other parts of Turkey in relative comfort. Dependence on extended and authoritarian families, local notables, and tribal ties restricted the growth of individualism. Dependent personalities basically made a lateral transition into another tribe— this time, however, a political tribe, namely the PKK. This organization reinvented "Kurdishness" in uniting its Kurdish recruits from different tribal affiliations and religious

---

[20] *Milliyet*, 11.11.1998.

denominations. Armed action forged an unprecedented sense of unity among Kurds with differing allegiances, as the organization directed them against a common enemy, namely the Turkish Republic, which was demonized as a colonizing power. Fighting against the "enemy" eradicated internal cleavages among PKK supporters which had always haunted Kurdish society, and forged an all-embracing organization, which replaced every other reality its members had left behind.

These factors made the PKK sacrosanct and beyond question for its adherents. The organization provided a livelihood and a cause to live and die for with dignity—something that most of the local youth lacked. Young women in particular found in the PKK ranks a means of emancipation from traditional bondage, and elevation to a status of equality with men. That partly explains why more women took part in suicide missions. The PKK was more than an organization for them; it provided a lifestyle, which, alas, was only a virtual reality.

The guts and glory story began to crumble in the mid-1990's, as the organization retreated in the face of Turkey's security forces and the world remained reluctant to afford it legitimate political identity. Suicide bombings were staged to boost morale and to show the organization's capacity for sacrifice and loyalty to its "cause." It was also a cry of desperation to the world community for help. Just as it had started, the suicide campaign ended by executive order. But the bombers had gone on historical record as the first to use the suicide method in challenging Turkey's political stability. Might other terrorist groups try to emulate them and adopt this form of violence? That remains to be seen.

Suicide Terrorism in Lebanon

Dr. Shaul Shay
ICT Research Fellow

I would like to open my presentation with a short discussion of the religious origins and background of Shi'ite suicide terrorism. Suicide terrorism as an act of martyrdom can be traced back fourteen centuries to the battle of Karbala. The Prophet's death in 632 C.E. left the Muslim community without clear guidelines for choosing a successor. The orthodox Sunnis accepted the reign of the temporal leaders, the Caliphs, whereas the Shi'ites believed their Imams were the divinely inspired and infallible descendants of Mohammed. In 680, Hussein, the son of Ali, cousin of Mohammed, and his wife Fatima, daughter of Mohammed, challenged the Sunni leader, Muravia. With his army outnumbered, Hussein marched to his certain death in the battlefield near Karbala, which is today in Iraq. To this day, passion plays and mass processionals are performed in the Shi'ite communities in Iran, Iraq, and Lebanon to commemorate this act. The ceremonies take place every year on *Ashura*, the tenth day of the month of *MU.K.hara*.

The Ayatolla Khomeini's revolution in Iran in 1979 changed the traditionally passive attitude of the Shi'ia. Khomeini called for Shi'ite activism and revolutionary violence against the enemies of Islam in the Muslim world and against the superpowers—mainly the U.S., but also the U.K., France, and Israel. While Orthodox Islam forbids the taking of one's own life, Khomeini was the first to provide religious justification for self-sacrifice for the sake of just and legitimate Islamic goals. Khomeini saw in Hussein's self-sacrifice at Karbala a model for each and every Shi'ite. All should be ready for self-sacrifice in the cause of Islam.

The Iran-Iraq war and the zealous drive to export the revolution provided the background for the phenomenon of hundreds and thousands of volunteers who committed acts of self-sacrifice on the battlefield with Iraq.

Assisted and inspired by the Iranian Revolutionary Guards, the Hizballah was established in Lebanon in 1983, and shortly afterwards became the first organization to introduce suicide terrorism into the Lebanese theater. In the early Eighties, the religious leadership of the Hizballah, mainly Sheik Fadlallah, the spiritual leader, accepted Khomeini's more activist doctrine after an internal debate on the moral and religious aspects of self-sacrifice. As a relatively small organization, the Hizballah was, and still is today, sensitive to casualties and the lives of its members. Therefore acts of self-sacrifice need to be justified by their cost-effectiveness.

On the 18th of April, 1983, a terrorist driving a van loaded with approximately 400 pounds of explosives rammed into the American Embassy in Beirut, killing 63 people and injuring many more. The Islamic Jihad, a name sometimes used by Hizballah, claimed responsibility for the attack. It was the first, but not the last, suicide terror attack in the Lebanese theater. Six months later, suicide bombers acting for the same terrorist group drove trucks loaded with explosives into U.S. Marine headquarters in Beirut and the French forces' headquarters, also in the Beirut area. And a few months later, another suicide bomber hit the IDF headquarters in Tyre.

This first wave of suicide bombings was the most significant and went some way towards achieving one of the key strategic goals of Hizballah and Iran: the evacuation of foreign forces from Lebanon. All the targets in this first wave were major command centers, and the attacks were cost-effective from the terrorists' point of view.

During the years 1985 and 1986 the situation in Lebanon changed. The IDF withdrew from the Beirut area and other parts of Lebanon, and created a new Security Zone north of the international border. The command centers and the camps moved south and the Hizballah changed tactics. In this period most of the suicide bombings were directed against IDF convoys in South Lebanon.

In the period between 1986 and 2000, the Hizballah declared war on the Security Zone. Suicide bombings were carried out mainly against front-line targets in the Security Zone, especially checkpoints and entry posts. But there were also suicide bombings against targets in the Security Zone itself. This type of attack required local infrastructure in the Security Zone; intelligence on IDF routines, convoys and activities; and the ability to smuggle explosives into the area, to prepare the car bomb and the suicide bomber for the mission.

Looking at the statistics, we see that in 1985-1986 new elements joined the "suicide terrorist club" in Lebanon. They included pro-Syrian organizations, which for a while took the lead in suicide bombings. The most important of these were the Syrian National Party, the PAS, the Lebanese Communist Party, and the Socialist Nasserist Party. All four were guided, trained, and operated by the Syrians. Most of their missions failed, but it was the first time that non-religious organizations like the Syrian National Party had launched a campaign of suicide bombings.

Again, looking at the statistics, we see that there were three basic periods: The first was the wave of suicide bombings carried out by the Hizballah in 1983. The second was the period between '85 and '86, when the Security Zone was created, and most of the attacks were by the pro-Syrian organizations. And then from '87 onwards, Hizballah again took the lead.

I would like to say a few words about the main characteristics of the suicide bombings in the Lebanese theater. Firstly, in most cases the terror activity was carried out by a single suicide bomber, of course with the logistic, operational, and intelligence support of a network or a cell. In most cases the suicide bomber was a male of between 17 and 30 years of age. But we know of at least five cases in which attacks were carried out by female bombers, mainly in the pro-Syrian organizations. The suicide bombers often used trucks or cars loaded with between 150 and 900 kilograms of explosives, but in some cases they carried the explosives in a belt or bag strapped to the body, very similar to the *modus operandi* used in Sri Lanka. There were a few cases in which suicide bombers used animals, mainly donkeys loaded with explosives, which they led up to the target, blowing themselves up together with the animal. There were also three or four cases of naval suicide bombings, in which boats loaded with explosives were used. Three of these attempts were carried out by Palestinian organizations, and one by the Syrian National Party.

If we analyze the statistics, we see that about half of the suicide events in Lebanon were carried out by Shi'ite organizations, mainly the Hizballah, but there were also a few Amal operations, mainly in the early Eighties. After a while the Hizballah changed a key element of its policy: Initially, it had taken responsibility for suicide attacks under the name of the Islamic Jihad, but it later accepted responsibility directly in its own name.

The Hizballah had introduced suicide bombing into the Lebanese theater in 1983. There were four cases that year, and it was the most significant and successful campaign of suicide terrorism in this region. From 1983 onwards, Hizballah carried out no more than one or two suicide attacks a year; in some years, even fewer. The later attacks from the mid-Eighties were less effective and caused fewer casualties. We also believe that the Hizballah was responsible for most of the operations classified as "perpetrators unknown." Small pro-Syrian organizations were responsible for 23 suicide bombings. Of this number, 16 were carried out by the Syrian National Party. Palestinians were responsible for 2 to 3 naval suicide bombing attempts, using boats loaded with explosives.

Looking at the overall figures, pro-Syrian organizations carried out 23 attempts. Hizballah, together with Amal carried out another 23, and if we add the "unknowns" to this category, we get about 26 Shi'ite suicide bombing attempts in Lebanon. In other words, in the years between 1983 and 2000 there were more than 50 suicide bombings in Lebanon.

From the statistical point of view, suicide bombings constituted less than 0.1 percent of overall terror activities in Lebanon. For instance, in 1999 there were about 1500 Hizballah operations in Lebanon; only one was a suicide attack. The suicide bombings caused relatively high numbers of casualties, as was evident mainly in the first wave against large, static targets in '83-'84. Later on, even though the total number of suicide attacks was much greater, the results were less painful and significant. But there is something more important than sheer numbers that we shouldn't overlook: despite the relatively low number of suicide attacks, they had great psychological impact; and suicide terrorism became a Shi'ite symbol that is still potent.

From 1986 onwards, the effectiveness of the suicide bombings was reduced by various countermeasures and tactics employed by the IDF and the SLA, and this is perhaps the main reason the casualties were much lower than in previous years. Suicide bombings, from the terrorist point of view, became less cost-effective compared to other methods, such as sophisticated roadside-bombs, booby-traps, explosive devices, ambushes and guided anti-tank missiles. Therefore, suicide bombing remained a unique tool for special occasions, mainly when the organization felt itself under pressure or when it needed to send a painful political and military message.

In conclusion, we can say that the Hizballah was the inspiration in the Lebanese theater and in the wider Middle Eastern arena for suicide terrorism. Both secular pro-Syrian organizations in Lebanon and Palestinian organizations like the Islamic Jihad and the Hamas adopted the model. It is also worth mentioning that the Hizballah also carried out suicide terrorism outside the Lebanese theater in different places in the world.

The last painful reminder of the Hizballah's capacity for suicide terrorism was on the 30th of December, 1999. The target was an IDF convoy near the village of Kleah, and the suicide bomber, in a Chevrolet car, blew himself up near the convoy. In this case, as a result of the convoy's correct operational procedure, there were not too many casualties; but it was a strong reminder that the Hizballah has the operational experience, the capacity, and enough potential volunteers, that a new campaign of suicide terrorism is only a question of decision.

Suicide Attacks in Israel

Boaz Ganor

Executive Director, International Policy Institute for Counter-Terrorism

Over the past decade, several countries all over the world have been forced to contend with the phenomenon of suicide attacks. Radical activists from such diverse countries as Turkey, Sri Lanka, Lebanon, as well as Palestinians, have elected to use suicide as a weapon in terrorist attacks aimed at various targets—both civilian and military—where large crowds tend to gather.

Suicide attacks constitute an additional stage in the escalation of terrorist activity, with the clear intention of causing the maximum number of casualties and damage—and even more importantly, of striking a blow to public morale.

What is a Suicide Attack?

A suicide attack is an "operational method in which the very act of the attack is dependent upon the death of the perpetrator." The terrorist is fully aware that if he does not kill himself, the planned attack will not be implemented. The attack is carried out by activating explosives worn or carried by the terrorist in the form of a portable explosive charge, or planted in a vehicle he is driving.

It is important to correctly define a suicide attack, for there are different types of attacks that may be mistakenly considered as belonging to this special category:

On many occasions, the perpetrator of an attack sets out with the knowledge that there is a good chance of being killed in the course of an attack (for example in trying to force a bus over a cliff). In spite of the imminent danger to the terrorist's life, as long as there is a possibility of the attack being carried out without his being forced to kill himself during the course of it, this should not considered to be a "suicide attack."

Sometimes the terrorist makes concrete preparations for the possibility of death as a result of the attack (preparing a will, carrying out purification ceremonies, etc.). However, these preparations in themselves do not turn the attack into a suicide attack.

In some attacks, the terrorists are equipped with arms or explosives for blowing themselves up should the attack go wrong—for example, if the attack fails, or security forces break into a building where terrorists are holding hostages. The existence of such arms or explosives—and even the decision use them—does not constitute adequate grounds for the attack to be defined as a suicide attack.

As mentioned above, in a true suicide attack, the terrorist knows full well that the attack *will not be executed* if he is not killed in the process.

The phenomenon of suicide attacks in Israel (within the '67 borders), developed simultaneously while the Middle East peace process was getting under way. The fundamentalist terrorist organizations—"Hamas" and the "Palestinian Islamic Jihad"—chose to make extensive use of suicide tactics in an attempt to undermine the Israeli public's sense of security.

The use of suicide attacks in Israel quickly became a widespread phenomenon, chiefly because of the new deployment of IDF in Gaza and the West Bank, which caused a decline in Israeli intelligence measures and operational ability. The phenomenon was abetted by the official Israeli response to these attacks, which disregarded the responsibility of the Palestinian Authority in preventing them.

Prior to the establishment of the Palestinian Authority, Palestinian organizations executed terrorist attacks against Israel whenever their operational ability allowed. Their capacity was limited only by the activity of Israeli security forces in the territories under Israeli control.

Following the establishment of the Palestinian Authority and the withdrawal of the IDF from the autonomous zones, Palestinian terrorist organizations could now deploy in areas "protected" from the Israeli Security Apparatus. This enabled them to consolidate, gain strength, and greatly increase their ability to execute terror attacks against Israel. From that point onwards, the factor actually limiting the scope of terrorist attacks against Israel in general, and the number of suicide attacks in particular, was no longer the operational capability of the organizations, but rather the motivation of these organizations to engage in attacks or refrain from them. (Their will to execute or refrain is influenced by the peace process, Israeli policy towards the Palestinian authority, operative steps on the part of Israel against the terrorist organizations, and—perhaps most of all—the attitude of the Palestinian public toward this kind of attack).

In implementing this wave of suicide attacks in Israel, Hamas and Islamic Jihad activists adopted the same tactics previously used by pro-Iranian and pro-Syrian groups in Lebanon.

The deportation to Lebanon of hundreds of fundamentalist Islamic activists from Gaza and the West Bank in 1992 greatly contributed to the new wave of suicide terrorism. The deportees received operational and military training from their comrades— Hizballah and their Iranian trainers. The decision to let them come back to their homes in Gaza and the West Bank after spending a year in Lebanon made it possible for the wave of suicide terrorism to grow and flourish in the Palestinian Authority.

Since 1993, 25 suicide attacks have been carried out (under the definition above) resulting in 156 dead and approximately 1200 wounded. (This includes the attack on The Apropo Cafe in Tel Aviv in March '97, which probably was not originally intended to be a suicide attack). Seventy-two percent of the attacks were executed by Hamas activists, compared to 28% by the Palestinian Islamic Jihad. Most of these attacks (16 in number) were carried out against Israeli civilian buses and public transportation targets. 60% of the attacks were carried out by bombers working alone or in pairs. These attackers carried the devices on their bodies or in suitcases. In 40% of the attacks a car bomb was used by the terrorists.

This data includes only suicide attacks that actually occurred, and not planned attacks or attacks that were thwarted by Israeli or Palestinian security forces.

Benefits of the suicide attack for the terrorist organization

Suicide attacks are attractive to terrorist organizations, as they offer them a variety of advantages:

First – Suicide attacks result in many casualties and cause extensive damage.

Second – Suicide attacks attract wide media coverage. A suicide attack is a newsworthy event for the media, as it indicates a display of great determination and inclination for self-sacrifice on the part of the terrorists.

Third – *Although a suicide attack is a very primitive and simple attack,* the use of suicide tactics guarantees that the attack will be carried out at the most appropriate time and place with regard to the circumstances at the target location. This guarantees the maximum number of casualties, in contrast to the use of technical means such as a time bomb or even a remote controlled explosive charge. In this regard, the suicide bomber is no more than a sophisticated bomb—a carrier that brings the explosive device to the right location and detonates it at the right time.

Fourth – In a suicide attack, as soon as the terrorist has set off on his mission his success is virtually guaranteed. It is extremely difficult to counter suicide attacks once the terrorist is on his way to the target; even if the security forces do succeed in stopping him before he reaches the intended target, he can still activate the charge and cause damage. (Thus the need for accurate intelligence concerning the plans of the terrorist organizations is crucial).

Fifth – Planning and executing the escape route after a terror attack has occurred is usually one of the most complicated and problematic aspects of any terrorist attack. Suicide attacks require no escape plan.

Sixth – Since the perpetrator is killed during the course of the suicide attack, there is no fear of his being caught afterwards, being interrogated by the security forces, and passing on information liable to endanger other activists.

Benefits for the perpetrator of the suicide attack

Suicide attacks are considered attractive by groups of religious and nationalistic fanatics who regard them as a kind of "holy war" and a divine command. The perpetrator of the suicide attack is not considered either by himself, by other activists or, in our case, by the Palestinian public at large, to have committed suicide. He is, rather, seen ase a "shahid"—a martyr who fell in the process of fulfilling a religious command, the "Jihad" or "holy war." (Thus his act is called in Arabic *Istishhad*).

Suicide attacks may provide the shahid and his family with substantial rewards:

First – The majority of the shahids come from a low-social-status background. The shahid improves his social status after his death, as well as that of his families.

Second – The family of the shahid is showered with honor and praise, and receives financial rewards for the attack—usually some thousands of dollars.

In addition to the religious mission,and the family rewards, the shahid also receives some personal benefits (according to his belief), including:

- Eternal life in paradise,
- The permission to see the face of Allah,
- And the loving kindness of 72 young virgins who will serve him in heaven.

The shahid also earns a privilege to promise a life in heaven to 70 of his relatives.

The will of Hisham Ismail Abd-El Rahman Hamed (a suicide attacker who blew himself up in November 1994 at Nezarim, killing 3 IDF officers and wounding 2 Israelis and 4 Palestinians) reflects the state of mind of the shahid at the time of the attack. He wrote:

> Dear family and friends! I write this will with tears in my eyes and sadness in my heart. I want to tell you that I am leaving and ask for your forgiveness because I decided to see Alla' today

and this meeting is by all means more important than staying alive on this earth…. (Maariv 13/11/94 p. 15)

Another suicide attacker – Salah Abed El Hamid Shaker, who blew himself up with another shahid at Beit Lid in January '95, killing 18 Israelis and wounding 36, wrote in his will:

I am going to take revenge upon the sons of the monkeys and the pigs—the Zionist infidels and the enemies of humanity. I am going to meet my holy brother Hisham Hamed and my distinguished teacher, Hani El Abed, and all other Shahids and saints in paradise. Please Forgive me." (Maariv, 23/1/95)

All of these factors constitute a substantial incentive for fundamentalist believers to adopt suicide attack tactics. When there are religious, nationalistic, economic, social, and personal rewards for this kind of action, it is no wonder that Hamas and Islamic Jihad find no difficulty in recruiting volunteers for such missions.

Benefits of the Suicide Attack

To the Organization

- Many casualties
- Media coverage
- Precisely-chosen time and place
- Guaranteed success
- No need for escape route

To the Terrorist

Personal image:

- Fulfillment of a religious commandment
- Partriotism

Personal benefits:

- Eternal life in Paradise
- 72 young virgins
- Privilege to promise life in heaven to 70 relatives

Family benefits:

- Social status improvement
- Economic improvement

Who is the shahid?

The common characteristics of the shahid, which serve as a basic profile of the suicide bomber, are the following:

- Young—usually from 18 to 27 years of age.
- Usually not married, unemployed and from a poor family.
- Usually the shahid completed high school.
- Most were devoted students in the Islamic fundamentalist education centers in Gaza and in the West Bank directed and financed by Hamas.
- Some of the shahids arrested by Israel in the past have expressed the desire to avenge the death or injury of a relative or a close friend at the hands of Israel.

The reason for committing a suicide attack for most of the shahids is therefore first and foremost religious fanaticism, combined with nationalist extremism and a wish for revenge, but not personal despair.

Usually a shahid does not volunteer for his missions. The shahid may be selected by his Islamic religious teacher at the mosques and Islamic education centers in Gaza and the West Bank. Usually the most devoted students are selected after a close examination by the teachers and over a long time of acquaintance. Sometimes the Shahid is picked by the planner or the initiator of the attack on the basis of previous acquaintance.

After the potential shahid is selected, he usually participates in long training sessions in order to test his attitudes and performance under pressure and in life-threatening situations. Only those trainees who are both willing and cool-headed are permitted to move on to the next stage.

Subsequently the shahid usually "disappears" from his home without farewell, while he begins several days of intensive training in order to understand all operational aspects of his mission and learn how to deal with the explosive device. At this time the shahid also undergoes a process of physical and mental purification.

Some captured terrorists who were trained to be shahids testified that at this stage they were taken to a graveyard and told to lie down inside one of the graves for several hours in order to overcome the fear of death. (*Yediot* 9/3/95), (*Maariv*, 24/3/97)

On the last day before the attack, the shahid is well-trained, brainwashed, and willing and able to execute the suicide attack. At his point he writes a will, in which he asks his family not to mourn him, because he did not die but rather was transformed to another life in which he will be with Allah. Also, he records a

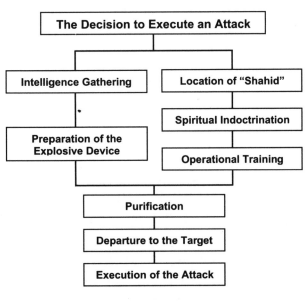

propaganda videocassette in which he is disguised (usually by wearing an IDF uniform or typical Israeli clothes and shaving his beard), he says a special prayer, and together with his collaborators he drives to the target area.

The shahid usually transports the explosive in a vehicle, sometimes even by bicycle or cart. Alternatively, the device may be hidden in a bag or in a military vest under a coat.

Standard explosives run to about 3-15 kilograms of TNT or homemade explosives. In order to increase the damage, small chunks of iron or a large quantity of nails are often packed around the explosives. The detonator is of a very simple design that allows the perpetrator to activate the explosives at the proper time even when under pressure.

How can we fight suicide terrorism?

Terrorists use suicide attacks to instill a feeling of helplessness in the target population—the notion that they have no way of protecting themselves against such attacks. These feelings strike a blow to public morale, creating fear and panic.

Any country faced with a struggle against this type of terrorism must do its utmost to protect the population, and to provide them with a feeling that "things can and will be done" against suicide attacks, in order to decrease the damage to public morale.

What then should be done in order to thwart suicide attacks? A state faced with suicide attacks must fight these attacks through intelligence, operational (counter-terrorist) measures, and protective (anti-terrorist) measures. To these steps must be added psychological measures.

Intelligence is the first link in the chain of combating any terror attack, but is of the utmost importance in thwarting suicide attacks before they are put into practice. The wave of suicide attacks in Israel in the Nineties reflects a decrease in Israeli intelligence capability against the terrorist organizations.

Operational (counter-terrorist) measures – Since direct action against the shahid himself is usually a complicated operation, operational efforts should be diverted towards the application of pressure on those elements involved in the overall planning and implementation of these attacks.

Surrounding the shahid are several circles of activists, who are aware in advance of the plan to execute a suicide attack.

The first circle is his family. In many cases they notice a change in the behavior of the shahid. In some cases the shahid has a brother or a father serving in the Palestinian security services, and this relative could report to his commanders and prevent the attack.

The second circle includes activists who initiate the attack, recruit the terrorist, train him, devise the explosive device, gather operational intelligence on the target, and guide the shahid on his mission.

The third circle is comprised of the collaborators, who give logistical assistance to the shahid and the operational team, and drive the shahid to the target.

And the last circle is the supporters who approve this kind of attack and create an atmosphere which makes it possible for the shahid and his team to operate freely among them.

The operational measures must focus simultaneously on all of these circles of activists.

Circles Around the Suicide Terrorist

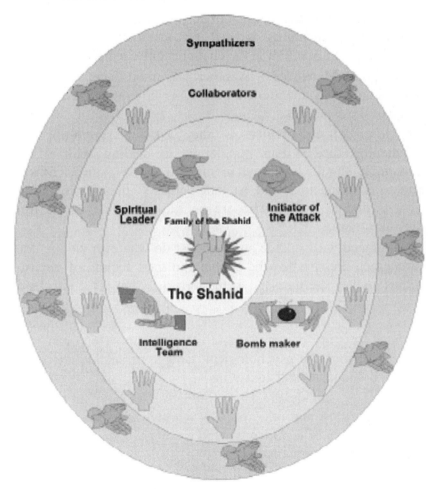

Security (Anti-Terrorist) Measures – Intelligence and operational measures alone are not sufficient. New security methods should be adopted, and action should be taken in order to prevent the Shahid from reaching his target or getting inside his target.

Even a shahid may be deterred, or at least his plans may be obstructed. Increased protective measures, and the exposure of the Shahid before he has the opportunity to carry out the attack at the planned target, may reduce the amount of damage caused by the Shahid and perhaps even prevent the attack.

The security measures are the last link in the chain of thwarting terror attacks. But in the absence of sufficient intelligence or where the operational capability against the terrorists is limited, the importance of this last link in the chain becomes exceedingly high.

Psychological Measures – Another important facet of fighting suicide attacks, as mentioned before, is countering the morale damage of these attacks.

Of foremost importance is the task of supporting and strengthening the civilian population in dealing with suicide terrorism. It should be borne in mind that the main victims of terrorism in general, and suicide attacks in particular, are civilians—and it is they who are on the front line in the fight against terrorism.

States faced with suicide attacks must do whatever can be done to strengthen the spirit of the people and their feeling of security, and thus convey the message to the terrorists that these attacks do not serve their goals. In this regard there must be cooperation between the administration, the media, decision-makers, politicians, security personnel, and other sectors which can work together to lessen the psychological damage of suicide attacks by means of propaganda and education.

In summary, suicide attacks are the latest "fashion" in terrorism in the Middle East and other regions worldwide. However, just as in the past waves of terrorism waxed and waned, so too this wave of terrorism will eventually die out.

In contending with the phenomenon of suicide terrorism, we should bear in mind that the suicide attack is not an act of a lone lunatic or desperate terrorist who decides to attack as an act of revenge. Rather, it is a well-planned terror attack, which demands extensive preparations and the involvement of a number of activists and leaders.

Therefore, countering this wave of terrorism requires a combination of effective intelligence, operational activity, security, and psychological measures, combined with international cooperation in the fight against the organizations responsible for such attacks.

Psychological and Sociological Dimensions of Suicide Terrorism

Session Chairman: Prof. Barry Rubin,
Deputy Director, BESA Center for Strategic
Studies, Bar Ilan University, Israel

The Views of Palestinian Society on Suicide Terrorism

Dr. Khalil Shiqaqi

Center for Palestine Research and Studies, Nablus, Palestinian Authority

In this article, we shall turn from studying the actor to studying the audience—from looking at the suicide bomber to looking at the society. What I am talking about is how Palestinian society perceives suicide attacks. I will discuss violence in general, but the focus will be on what motivates people to support or to oppose suicide attacks, rather than what motivates people to commit them.

To support or oppose violence and suicide attacks is of course a matter of policy preference. As a society, societies make policy preferences all the time. They support the peace process or they support violence. If they choose violence, they support violence against military targets or violence against civilians. And when they support violence against civilians, sometimes they support violence against the civilian collective, and sometimes only against individual civilians. The question that I will try to address is, what determines those policy preferences? Why do   ople support or oppose violence and suicide attacks?

Remember, Palestinian society is very traditional. It is both Muslim and traditional. There is a religious prohibition against suicide. Moreover, as a traditional society, it does not encourage individualism. Remember also, what Durkheim, the French sociologist said—"individualism leads to suicide." So, for both religious and social reasons, we should not expect to see suicide attacks, or support for them, among Palestinians.

I have three themes I want to develop. The first is that support for violence among Palestinians is dependent on the Palestinian perception of the threat posed to them by Israel or Hamas. In other words, the issue we need to examine is the threat-perception. Threat-perception is an emotional issue. The more intense the perception of threat, the more likely the selection of a more extreme policy preference. And in terms of what forms of violence a society will support, suicide attacks top the list as the highest form of violence in terms of intensity. According to my thesis, this *modus operandi* requires of its supporters the highest degree of threat-perception at the emotional level.

My second theme relates to cost-benefit calculations. This is a more rational matter. We have to consider the aftermath of the violence of suicide attacks. Does it lead anywhere? Does it alleviate suffering? Does it mitigate the threat-perception, or does it create more problems? While one can deduce policy decisions in terms of how to fight suicide attacks, it is not very easy to do so. There is no simple causal relationship here.

The reason for this is that the threat to vital values and needs is sometimes posed not by those who actually cause the threat-perception, but by those who try to mitigate it. So, in our case, the Israelis, by their behavior, may cause a perception of threat. And that may lead to support for violence and suicide attacks. Then the suicide bombers might, by their actions, cause certain policy preferences on the Israeli side, which impose costs on Palestinian society. That society will then have to decide whether it wants to support suicide attacks, given the knowledge of the cost. This is where the cost-benefit calculations come into the picture. Remember, though, it is not a simple cost-benefit calculation. It is also an emotional reaction to threat.

Policy preference

Let me very quickly define my dependent variable. This is of course the policy preference—should I or should I not support violence, and should I or should I not support suicide attacks? The policy here in our case is a matter of three choices. I can support the highest form of violence, which is suicide attacks. Here the problems are that I target civilians, the Israeli collective, and I kill myself—three things at once. This is in contrast to less extreme, medium-intensity violence, which would entail support for attacks against civilians, but not necessarily against the collective; and where I do not necessarily kill myself in the process. The third possibility would be simply to support attacks against Israelis—mainly military targets, but also, from time to time, attacks on civilians.

The point of departure is that you are fighting back against forces of oppression, the military in particular. But you know, in our case, Palestinians do not see a great deal of difference between settlers and the military, although they do distinguish very clearly between civilians inside Israel, and the military and settlers.

Independent variables

My independent variables are the perception of threat and the cost-benefit calculations. I would say there are five basic components of this threat as perceived by the Palestinians, and if you have most of these components, then the intensity of threat-perception is likely to be very high. But again, as you can see in some of the components, their introduction sometimes actually reduces the intensity.

The most important component in my view is the threat to life, particularly when seen as a threat to the collective life of Palestinians. This was the case in the Baruch Goldstein massacre in Hebron. It is a most important example.

The second most important factor is the threat to land. Land is a very important value in the Palestinian perception, so Israeli settlement activities are a cause for threat. Israel's confiscation of land and its failure to re-deploy from parts of the West Bank and Gaza could also cause Palestinians to feel threatened.

The third component in the threat-perception is a threat to political values and needs. And here one can actually have some contradictory tendencies. On the one hand, there are those who oppose the peace process and want to terminate it. And there are those who think that the peace process will lead to the end of occupation, and would therefore see a threat to the peace process as a threat to their values. State-building is also a political value, and threats to state building from within give rise to the threat of civil war. Is Hamas trying to push us into civil war or is the Palestinian

Authority pushing us in that direction? Are the Israelis preventing the Palestinians from achieving sovereignty, etc.? These are basic political values, and when Palestinians feel a threat to these values, again that will affect their policy preferences.

A fourth component is the threat to religious and traditional values. Anything that affects Jerusalem immediately causes an emotional response, and we have seen that in cases such as the opening to tourism of the tunnel excavations beneath the Western Wall in 1996.

Finally, there is an economic component in the form of threats against the standard of living—issues preventing employment, free movement of goods and labor. This particular component is in fact inconsistent with the other components, and it is here that the cost-benefit calculations come in. But this is not the only factor in cost-benefit calculations. Remember the impact of suicide or other major attacks in our own Palestinian or Arab history. Go back to the period after the Lebanese war when the Americans were hit in Lebanon and then the Israelis were hit in some places in the south of Lebanon. The American response was to leave immediately and the Israelis re-deployed to a smaller zone, and now they want to get out of that too.

If you want to consider the importance of violence, you have to consider what comes next. In the Palestinian case, after the violence of 1996, the result was a new right-wing Israeli government. There was also a great deal of closure of the Palestinian territories that went back in fact to 1994-1995. Therefore, we have a mixed bag of cost-benefit calculations and expectations as to where violence might lead. Will it force withdrawal as in the Lebanon case, or will it lead to clamp-down and the emergence of a right-wing Israeli government as in the Palestinian case of '94-'96?

Historical development

In order to explain what has been happening, I want to take you through the stages of how the Palestinians have perceived this historically, and I mean in the past 6 to 7 years. Let's look at four stages of the Palestinian response to threat-perception. The first stage is the 1993 phase. There was a great deal of expectation on the part of the Palestinians. I do not have figures here to show how much support there was for violence, as we do not have data covering the 1993 period. My guess, though, is that, given this picture of expectation and what followed, the support for violence at this stage was generally low. And I would guess that there was little or no support whatsoever for suicide attacks. Why? The support for Oslo was 65%; willingness to amend the Palestinian Charter was very high at 57%; expectation that the economy would pick up and that there would be a major economic dividend was also very high at 65%. This was the first stage. It lasted for a very short time.

The second period was 1994 and the first half of 1995. This is a period marked by suicide attacks. In terms of incidents of attacks, this is the period that witnessed the highest number. What happened during this period? Well, first of all we have the Baruch Goldstein massacre. Second, we had Rabin continuing with settlement activities. Then we had stagnation in the peace process. Little progress was made. There was some progress from time to time, but overall this was not a time of great success in the peace process. Fourthly, we had a drop in support for the peace process to 51%. In fact, immediately after the Baruch Goldstein massacre, support for the peace process did not exceed 17%. We also had Fatah and the opposition almost equal in terms of public support. Fatah had fought as the mainstream Palestinian faction. Now the opposition had 40% and Fatah had 40%, so the balance of power in Palestinian society was almost equal. 20% were either undecided or unaffiliated. Arafat's popularity, at 44%, was, relatively speaking, very low. Support for violence in general was 57%, and support for suicide attacks was only slightly less. Normally support for overall violence would be much higher than for specific suicide attacks.

The third phase was the end of 1995 to early 1996. This is the period that Israelis remember most as being very brutal. There were several attacks in February and March 1996, in the run-up to the 1996 Israeli election. Now, what happened in this third phase? For Palestinians, by the way, this was the best phase of all, not because of the suicide attacks, but because of other things. For one, the Israelis had just re-deployed from major cities in the West Bank.

Yes, there was some bad news. There were the Ayash and Shiqaqi assassinations, but overall the picture was not bad in terms of how the general population perceived it. We also had the Rabin assassination, which was perceived positively in the sense that more Palestinians felt supportive of the peace process as a result, and not the other way around. Fourthly, we had support for the peace process at its highest level, with 80% of Palestinians supporting it during this period. Fifthly, we had Arafat's popularity going up from 44% in the earlier period to 65%, and Fatah's jumping from 40% to 55%. Support for violence and for those specific suicide attacks was at its lowest. In terms of overall theoretical support for suicide attacks, only 18% supported them. The actual suicide attacks of February and March received the support of only 21% of Palestinians.

Now I must remind you of the ever-present distinction between civilians and military. When we carried out this series of surveys, we did not ask whether Palestinians supported attacks on Israeli soldiers, but based on previous surveys and up to this point, support for attack on military targets would have been much higher, up to 70%. Nonetheless, this again stems from the policy preference. Only a feeling that you are extremely threatened would lead you, in my thesis, to support attacks against civilians, and then even suicide attacks. The major distinction between the two is that you kill yourself and, secondly, that you target a collective, and not just individual Israelis.

The fourth period can be called "The Netanyahu Period." This was the period after Netanyahu was elected, where we had a freeze in the peace process. There was also a lot of talk about settlements and going back to a settlement drive. Of course we had the tunnel incident just two months after Natanyahu's election. During this period support for overall violence went up to 45% or so.

We also had two important events that could affect the cost-benefit calculations. One was the September 1996 tunnel confrontation, in which more than 70 Palestinians and about 18

Israelis were killed, and we had a very bloody confrontation. What was the lesson from what happened in 1996? Remember, historically speaking, the September 1996 confrontation came just 3-4 months before the signing of the Hebron Agreement. In other words, the first progress in the peace process in the Netanyahu period followed a major violent confrontation. The second development was the beginning of talk of Israel withdrawing from Lebanon. Under pressure from the Hizballah, Netanyahu started speaking about withdrawing from Lebanon. At this point, cost-benefit calculations were again introduced into the calculations, and the increase in the level of support for violence in this period was not just an emotional response to threat. This increase in support for violence, though, was not as high as in the earlier second phase.

The last phase is what one might call "The Current Phase." We are beginning to see a reduction in the overall level of support for violence. It is not stable, and although one can probably understand what is happening, one waits to see what develops. We are talking about a very short period of time, and therefore it is very difficult to make any generalizations.

During this period we have had delays in the implementation of the Wye River accords and we have delays in the implementation of various stages of redeployment. We have had some problems, and the expectation is that there might be more problems. Support for the peace process is relatively high, somewhere between 73%-77%, not as high as the 80% peak, but certainly not low. We also have the Barak Government actually deciding to withdraw from Lebanon by a specific date. Again, cost benefit-calculations as well as emotional response come into the equation.

The overall level of support for violence today is somewhere between 35% and 45%. We have not had any suicide attacks yet, in which we could check how much of that support would carry over. My guess is that it would definitely be more than the 20% that we saw before, but that it would not be as high as it was during the Netanyahu period or the second phase in 1994. If I am right—if threat-perception and cost-benefit calculations are indeed behind the policy preference of support for violence in general, and the intensity of that threat-perception and the cost-benefit calculations lead to the decision as to what form of violence to support—then one would say that one's political affiliation is very important, because it represents political values.

Remember the components of the threat-perception. One would probably find that Hamas supporters are likely to support violence, while Fatah supporters are less inclined to do so. This goes without saying; the point is that it has to do with the political value component of the threat-perception. My figures indicate that support for violence and suicide attacks among Hamas supporters is consistent at approximately 70%, while among Fatah supporters it varies from time to time. The 1996 attacks produced only 14% support for the suicide attacks among Fatah supporters, versus the 70% or so among Hamas supporters—and therefore the threat to political values seems to be an important variable.

The second factor is awareness. You have to be aware of the threat to be able to be influenced by it, and in general you have to follow the news in order to be able to actually perceive the threats. And following the news is almost automatically, in our case, the product of education. As a result, the more educated you are, the more likely you are to support violence. The general world trend is precisely the opposite: the more educated you are, the less likely you are to support violence and suicide attacks. Here I can give you the figures for the 1996 suicide attacks. Only 13% of illiterate Palestinians supported these attacks. Among those who have a B.A. degree, the figure was 28%, more than double. There were also suicide attacks in Jerusalem in June and August of 1997, and there too the trend was similar. The current level of support for violence in general reflects the same trend, with 34% of the illiterates supporting violence versus 50% of those who have a university degree. Again the more educated you are, the more aware you are, and the more aware you are of events, the more likely you are to support violence.

Thirdly, there is the question of individual financial responsibility and cost-benefit calculation. For example, if you are a laborer in Israel, then you suffer the consequences of closures. If you are a merchant working in Israel, you also suffer the consequences. Therefore you are likely to be less willing than the general population to support violence, and definitely much less willing than those who have little responsibility and therefore do not care about the consequences—for example students or professional people who work within the Palestinian community, and will not be affected by closures. These are people who work within the community, and whose work does not depend on the Israelis. Again I can show you the figures. For the students, support for the suicide attacks of 1996 was 30%. The same goes for professionals. But of the merchants, only 20% supported the suicide attacks. As for the current level of support for general violence among Palestinians, students and professionals are in the 55%-60% range of support for violence, while laborers and merchants are in the 35%-40% range, again underlining the distinction. That is where the cost-benefit calculations come into the picture.

Let me give you just one more example of the importance of the cost-benefit calculations. Gaza, which used to be a very supportive of violence, is much less so today. Why? Because of the cost-benefit calculations. Gazans depend on work in Israel much more than West Bankers and therefore are more likely to be affected by punitive measures by Israel. Therefore, there is less support for violence and suicide attacks in Gaza.

Age is also a very important factor. The younger generation—those who do not yet need to work, or students—are much more supportive of violence than the older generation. And I can give you the breakdown by age. For the 1996 suicide attacks, of 45-50 year-olds, only 13% supported violence. For 18-22 year-olds, the level of support was 25%.

Cost-benefit calculations are also a factor in determining what to do about suicide attacks. Because the 1996 suicide attacks came during the third phase, in which Palestinians were extremely happy with the way things were going, a majority of about 60% supported the crackdown against Hamas. The PA, following these suicide attacks, arrested approximately 1,500 people off the streets, people who were implicated in the attacks. The Palestinian Authority also closed down many Hamas offices. We did not really expect to see that level of support for the PA crackdown. In fact, what makes things even more interesting is the fact that even though 75% of the people thought or feared that such a crackdown might lead to internal infighting, nonetheless a majority of about 60% continued to support it.

In conclusion, while I cannot demonstrate a clear causal relationship from the evidence, I can show a very clear correlation between threat-perception and support for violence. The more intense one's threat-perception, the more likely that one will support extreme responses. And the extreme in our case is suicide attacks.

Appendix

Policy Paper on Countering Suicide Terrorism

Following are the operative conclusions of the Conference on "Countering Suicide Terrorism" held by the International Policy Institute for Counter-Terrorism.

1. Suicide terrorism is one of the most extreme and indiscriminate methods used by terrorist groups. It threatens the lives of innocent people and bears destructive psychological and social consequences for the population at large. In many cases it makes perverse political use of religious, ethnic and nationalist ideologies in misleading people of faith and the general public.

2. Terrorism—and particularly suicide terrorism—is not merely a domestic problem affecting certain countries, but an international phenomenon that endangers the well being of whole populations.

3. In order to combat terrorism in general and suicide terrorism in particular, members of the international community must:

   a. Enhance the cooperation between people of all faiths in order to confront the misinterpretations of faith used by terrorist groups to justify suicide terrorism—an action which is in fact prohibited by all creeds.

   b. Fight the so-called religious legitimacy given to suicide terrorism by extremist groups and individuals, which present themselves as authoritative men of religion, by arousing public awareness to their intentions and misleading ideas.

   c. Lead an education campaign in the affected countries, aimed specifically for the young—who all too often become "cannon fodder" for the use of manipulative recruiters. This campaign should concentrate on countering the distortion of ideological and religious beliefs and should expose the real goals and dreadful consequences of such acts of terror.

   d. Dry up existing financial resources of terrorist organizations, and prohibit the raising of funds in the name of religious or social goals that will in fact be used to finance terrorist operations, or to fund propaganda activities used to create hatred between peoples or faiths.

e. Jointly develop new technologies and tactics, and strengthen special counter-terrorist units specialized in thwarting suicide attacks.

f. Expand existing cooperation between law-enforcement and intelligence agencies, and work to share expertise in confronting this phenomenon.

g. Establish international funds to be used for research in the field of countering suicide terrorism.

h. Formulate and enforce joint international policies against governments sponsoring, or actively participating in, terrorism and suicide terrorism.

i. Declare that no political goal justifies the use of terrorism (defined as an intentional violent attack on the lives of civilians in order to achieve political goals).

The participants in the International Conference on "Countering Suicide Terrorism," organized by The International Policy Institute for Counter-Terrorism, The Interdisciplinary Center, Herzliya, declare their support and commitment to the above declaration.

Herzliya, February 23, 2000